ECO
FASHION

ECO
FASHION

SASS BROWN

Laurence King Publishing

LAURENCE KING

Published in 2010 by
Laurence King Publishing Ltd
361–373 City Road
London EC1V 1LR
United Kingdom
email: enquiries@laurenceking.com
www.laurenceking.com

© text 2010 Sass Brown
Published in 2010 by Laurence King Publishing Ltd

A catalogue record for this book is available from the British Library.

ISBN: 978 1 85669 691 3

Design by Eleanor Ridsdale of Rudd Studio

Printed in China

Mixed Sources
Product group from well-managed
forests and other controlled sources
www.fsc.org Cert no. SGS-COC-003548
© 1996 Forest Stewardship Council

An innovator in environmental and socially sustainable
production, FIN's collection has a confident, careless
look with a hint of masculinity.

CONTENTS

FOREWORD

Above: This hand-dyed jacket by Geoffrey B. Small is made from summer cashmere and cotton jersey from Thiene in Vicenza, Italy, with a lining of patchworked vintage and new Italian luxury fabrics.

Left: Another jacket uses special interior lining patchwork in exclusive print pure silk, cotton and Bemberg viscose from Como, Italy.

The race is on. Fifty years ago earth held three billion people. Today, six billion. By 2050, it could be ten billion. By all estimates, there will not be enough resources for everyone. Water, food, energy and every material needed by man will be fought for, hoarded or protected from others. Deforestation, continuing unchecked carbon and methane gas emissions, drought and flooding driven by global warming, rampant consumerism and waste will all accelerate the reduction of available resources and make the problems spiral. The decline of fish stocks may mean there is virtually nothing left to fish by 2050. Already there is a world food crisis: one billion people are starving. Conflicts over water, food and energy are everywhere. Last year alone, one person in every 50 in the world lost their home due to war, earthquake, flood, fire, global warming disaster or foreclosure. And sneaking in through the back door as a solution to global warming is the looming spectre of a world nuclear energy renaissance now racing madly ahead with all its inherent apocalyptic dangers and totally unresolved risks. But if 'fashion reflects the times', you would be hard pressed to see it.

Fast fashion, planned obsolescence, ignorance and waste rule. In the UK last year, people threw away over two million tonnes of fast-fashion clothing that was worn an average of just six times. The mountains of plastic and polyester synthetic throwaway apparel are ending up in African landfills where they do not break down, water tables are disrupted and deadly new forms of malaria grow in the still ponds they create. Slave labour is rampant. The average factory-worker wage in the largest producing country for famous brand-name sport shoes is US$59 (£36) a month. Strikes are put down by soldiers. The use of cotton pesticides is huge and water consumption is enormous. More and more cancerous diseases are being attributed to our constant exposure to petrochemical-based products like plastic and polyester. Hazardous chemicals are now found in the bodies of all newborn babies.

Bad for the customer, bad for the worker, bad for society and bad for the environment, fashion today is one of the industrial age's biggest human failures. Dominated by large global corporate groups and their sponsored media who encourage a dream lifestyle of selfishness, apathy, superficiality, greed, sex and drugs to a growing worldwide audience of billions, fashion has been sold to the ratters, leaving its consumers and producers poorer, dumber and more ill-equipped than ever to face combat or survive the doomsday scenarios that everyone from religious fanatics to Nobel laureates predict will take place within a lifetime. Fashion is indeed a massive human, social and environmental disgrace in need of a paradigm shift.

That shift has begun. In the wake of the 2008 financial meltdown, we are witnessing the end of the industrial era as we know it and the collapse of the failed system behind it. Many large fashion corporations, which once dominated their marketplace by exploiting debt-burdened consumers buying on credit and workers in feudalistic conditions, are now reeling and on the brink of economic failure with no help in sight. The mighty rules of sustainability are now making themselves known to all.

And so, a book that for the very first time examines sustainability in fashion and a few of its pioneering practitioners, proponents and concepts is, indeed, a timely thing. Historic and courageous, its effort alone merits both immense applause and support for its author Sass Brown and its publisher Laurence King. With clothes covering the body and skin every day, and well over one trillion dollars a year in sales and at least half a billion people employed in the industry, few things in the world touch as many people as fashion, apparel and textiles. A new definition of fashion with a new set of values and a priority to get involved and develop real and fundamental solutions to the world's resource and lifestyle challenges, instead of promoting escapism and selfishness, could make the difference between world calamity and world improvement, between apocalypse and a better way of life for us all.

The choice is ours. Great fashion like great art, always 'reflects the times'. And it's truly a time for great fashion to appear. But time itself is of the essence. And what is at stake is our race.

As the late George Carlin used to joke, 'Everyone's running around screaming about the planet in danger – uh, the planet is going to be just fine, thank you, it's been around for hundreds of millions of years without a problem – it ain't the planet that's in danger – it's us.' Indeed. The race is on.

Geoffrey B. Small

SUSTAINABILITY IN FASHION

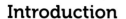

Left: Organic silk and ivory linen, featuring bustle-back styling, for the Elena García collection.

Centre: ModaFusion work with Brazilian cooperatives to produce a collection that uses traditional techniques and motifs paired with Parisian style.

Top: FIN's eco luxury collection is a homage to movement, with poetic and voluminous silhouettes produced in ecological fabrications.

Sustainability is the conservation of life through ecological balance – human, animal, vegetable and planetary. A self-sustaining system is a system that does not take more from the environment than it gives back; it does not deplete resources, but sustains itself. A pond or a forest is a sustainable system because it does not need anything to survive that it cannot reproduce or replace. So what is sustainable design? In clothing, it means sourcing and production that do not pollute through the process of manufacture and do not deplete non-renewable resources, whether those are planetary or human. It refers to clothing that can be absorbed back into the environment when it has reached the end of its life. Very few products, let alone garments, fulfil the concept of sustainability in its entirety.

A quiet revolution has been slowly growing in fashion since the outcry against sweatshop and under-age labour in the 1990s. The systemic growth of multinational branding, the anti-globalization movement, the AIDS pandemic, the growing inequities between rich and poor and the greater knowledge and communication of human rights' abuses, global warming, carbon dioxide emissions and polar ice caps melting all explain why many people feel the necessity to make a difference, in their life as well as in their work. We, the West, account for 5 per cent of the world's population, yet consume a quarter of the earth's energy.

The clothing and textile industry is one of the largest industries in the world, employing one sixth of the world's population. It uses more water than any other industry apart from agriculture. It discharges toxic chemicals into the environment, uses huge amounts of energy and is a major contributor to global warming. As a design community, we share the collective guilt of sweatshops, environmental pollution and child labour. As an industry, we lag behind the rest of the art and design community, where a significant number of architects, interior designers and cosmetic and fragrance companies base their business practices in ethical design. The industry traditionally satisfies itself with high-profile, red-carpet events that raise enormous amounts of cash, and which allow us as a community to collectively wash our hands of our responsibility to society and the sustainability of our planet, on an annual basis. The bleak concerns of *The Wall Street Journal's* Bob Ortega were quoted in his 1998 book, *In Sam We Trust*: 'In truth, the entire apparel industry was one continuing and under-reported scandal'.

The high-profile exposure of the current ecological state of the planet, once so hotly debated and denied by governments and scientists worldwide, is no longer in question, and is the major reason that ecology and social-outreach-based fashion design companies now cover all areas of design, from the fringe market to the mainstream and high-end arena. The current point of contention is not whether global warming is a reality, with 21 of the 22 hottest years on record occurring in the last 25 years, but how quickly water levels will rise due to the polar ice caps melting. Al Gore and others have estimated that to solve the problem of global warming, we must reduce carbon dioxide emissions by 60 to 80 per cent by 2050. Meanwhile, the US Department of Energy has calculated that the world's future energy needs will increase by 60 per cent by 2030. →

As with other social and political statements through commercial art, eco fashion is a reaction to social and ecological conditions.'

Left: Elena García's fine, organic, black silk tunic dresses were inspired by the iconic figures of Queen Victoria and Daphne Guinness.

Top: Inspired by the paintings of Andrew Wyeth, Camilla Norrback achieves a painterly quality in her ethereal subdued styling.

Above: An artisan hand finishes a piece for the Royah collection at the atelier in Afghanistan.

This is the immediate message heard by millions worldwide, and the reason many individuals and companies, including high-fashion corporations, are rushing in to make a difference while governments are still measuring, researching and debating. As with other social and political statements through commercial art, eco fashion is a reaction to social and ecological conditions. This is no longer a mess that 'our generation' is leaving for the next, but one that necessitates immediate action by everyone or else we will all experience the ramifications. Famine, wars, water shortages, disease and enforced migration are all forecast as the result of global warming. As Vivienne Westwood so eloquently said in an interview with Jonathan Ross in 2009, this is 'a price just too steep to pay'.

The idea of the artist as an activist is not a new one. Whether fine artists, musicians, writers, architects or designers, artists have always used their 'art' as a means of expression. Art and design have expressed political, cultural and social movements in all cultures across the centuries. Different cultures around the world have long indicated religious affiliations as well as dynastic lineage and rank through the use of colour, fabric and style in their dress codes. The modification of the traditional Chinese Sun Yat-sen suit, adopted as China's national dress by Mao Zedong, was an effort to assign revolutionary and patriotic significance to clothing. The Black Panthers adopted the black leather jacket, beret and narrow-leg trousers as a political and social statement of black solidarity and pride. The Sex Pistols, clothed by Vivienne Westwood and Malcolm McLaren, made a social, or rather, an anti-social statement through their clothing as much as their lyrics. Katharine Hamnett's '58% don't want Pershing' slogan T-shirt, which she so famously wore to Downing Street for her meeting with then British prime minister Margaret Thatcher, was a political statement.

The coming of age of ethical fashion has been a long time coming, and the road is littered with well-intentioned monstrosities and plain, boring and often downright ugly clothing. Only recently have fashion and ethics been able to coexist in the same sentence relatively comfortably. Picking through the plethora of ethical labels, the good, the well fitting and the fashionable are still few and far between, but nevertheless are growing in number and strength. The best and the brightest have earned a place in the fashion constellation. Noir, Linda Loudermilk and Geoffrey B. Small can all be judged against the best of the best from a purely aesthetic perspective and not come up short.

The growth of eco-friendly and socially conscious corporations continues to rise and move upmarket. The cool quotient associated with being earth friendly is also likely to increase as it becomes even more imperative to change the way we live and work for the very survival of our species. This will, of course, encourage more marketing campaigns and hollow gestures by many corporations eager to capitalize on the trend, but the genuine efforts of those who truly wish to make a difference in the ecology of our planet and the sustainability of human development will also proliferate.

This book honours what groundbreakers are doing in the fashion industry to integrate their concerns for our planet and the people on it into their business strategies. The designers and labels featured here herald change in the fashion industry, be that in the form of entirely new business models, recycling, reusing, redesigning, sustainable manufacturing processes, diversion of waste materials from landfill, fair trade or community development. This book is about good design that gives back. Good design in its many guises, from street fashion to couture and everything else in-between.

Chapter One

COMMUNITY & FAIR TRADE

Social capitalism is the outgrowth from non-governmental organizations (NGOs) around the world that use the cultural and historic skill sets of communities in developing nations as a means of building sustainable employment. Traditionally coordinated by social and cultural anthropologists, ecologists and social activists, these NGOs have attempted to compete with sophisticated global designers and labels with ethnic craft products. They have created small niche markets for these products, but usually have failed to develop global competitiveness; nevertheless, these traditional craft skills have become more valued and used, and eventually incorporated into the fashion industry through partnerships with high-end designers.

Fashion has often taken its inspiration from different countries and distinct communities around the world that use craft as a recognizable element of their aesthetic. In the past, however, high-end design has rarely used the craft expertise of the communities it takes its inspiration from by incorporating those skills into the final product. Designers have preferred to copy the ideas, reinterpret them to better suit their market and produce them using Western industry standards. Fashion designers have recently woken up, however, to the rich diversity of global craft techniques, partnering with NGOs and community groups around the world to include their work in their designs, while simultaneously supporting their communities. There have always been import companies, bringing in Indian embroidered sundresses, African beaded jewellery and Peruvian knitted sweaters. The difference now is that these craft-based cooperatives are partners in the development and production of items based on their skill sets, but designed by an international partner or brand with a highly developed sense of the global aesthetic, allowing the cooperatives to compete in the sophisticated marketplace of luxury fashion. These partnerships are vastly different from the recent history of low-cost labour; instead, they honour the traditions and craft skills of their artisanal partners and build on them through their designs. The sample-making process in itself becomes a creative partnership, which cannot be dictated to and must allow for the myriad variations that occur from artisan to artisan and from craft to craft.

A special place is reserved for companies and designers that have not only been inspired by the rich diversity of global craft skills, but that also incorporate the sustainability of the communities that inspire their work into their business model. With the eradication of traditional craft talent in the developed nations of North America and Western Europe, a greater appreciation has developed for the indigenous and inherited craft expertise in communities around the world. Many companies have chosen to build their companies in tandem with the communities they are in partnership with, including development, educational and health programmes in their long-term plans.

Noir in Denmark is in partnership with Ugandan farmers and supports their development and production of organic long-staple cotton. Carla Fernandez of Taller Flora works with Mexican artisans, reinterpreting their techniques into highly sophisticated designs while learning from their knowledge: a truly collaborative process. With every design and every stitch, Alabama Chanin honours the women of the south of the USA, their history, their struggles and their everyday skill sets. Her work is a labour of love. These are just a few examples of the incredible work being produced in this area of design.

A layered fabric of single and two ply silk was used for this shawl, produced by Shoto Banerji, which was inspired by the wings of a bird.

ALABAMA CHANIN

After returning to the home of her grandparents, bordered by cotton fields and at the base of the Appalachian Mountains in Florence, Alabama, Natalie Chanin founded the company Project Alabama in 2000. Project Alabama came to be known for its elaborately embellished hand-sewn garments: At its height, it enlisted the craftsmanship of approximately 200 artisans, called 'stitchers', all living and working within a three-hour radius of Chanin's small ranch-style home. Her cottage-industry approach to business was touted as the way of the future. Yet, by 2006, Project Alabama had ceased to be, only to be replaced, like a phoenix from the ashes, by a new company called Alabama Chanin, which is based on the years of experience with Project Alabama.

Using mostly 100 per cent-cotton recycled T-shirts as a base, Alabama Chanin produces beautiful work-intensive pieces that have little in common with the humble origins of the second-hand T-shirt. Having developed techniques that combine tonal stencilling, fabric layering, naïve basting stitching, chain stitching and whip stitching with knotted ends, and cutting out patterns to reveal coloured layers of fabric beneath, Alabama Chanin creates elaborate, decorative and highly innovative designs. The simple well-fitted styling balances the complexity of the techniques and textures to produce some breathtaking effects. Chanin's garments range from deceptively simple T-shirts, made from combinations of patchwork, reverse appliqué and stencil printing, to elaborate beaded and embroidered multilayered party dresses and wedding dresses. Chanin explains, 'Most of the techniques are based on the quilting and embroidery techniques of the Depression-era South, and others have been practiced by artisans for hundreds of years. I have borrowed this knowledge and made it the foundation of most of my designs.' →

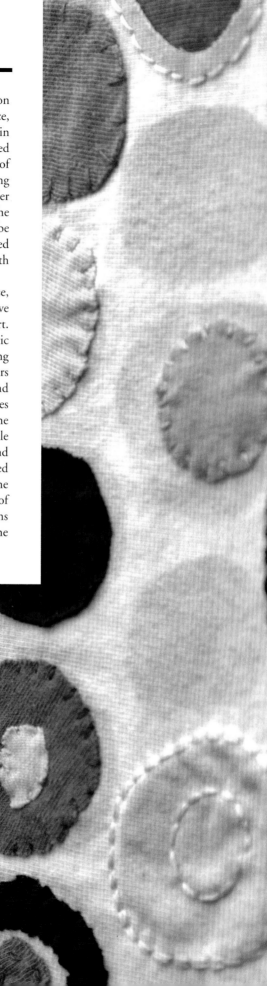

Alabama Chanin crafts limited-edition pieces made by hand and using a combination of new, organic and recycled materials. Designs are hand-appliquéd on top or cut away to reveal a second layer below.

'Living arts are an essential part of the social fabric of our communities, like planting seeds, reaping the fruits of our labors, and preserving our food.'

Chanin enlists the help of local quilters and seamstresses who grew up learning to sew at the feet of their grandmothers, mothers and aunts. For generations, the creation of sustainable products using materials readily available to them has been part of these women's everyday lives: they made quilts, knitted afghans, baked bread and stitched beautiful prom dresses. Chanin's fine appreciation of these skills, and the artisan inside us all, has led the creative direction of her company: 'At Alabama Chanin, we consider [our artisans'] work to be extraordinary, and we try to reclaim a time when products were made by hand by skilled artisans who played an esteemed role in their communities.'

Striving to preserve these fading domestic arts, Chanin puts them into a contemporary context. She sees their preservation as our connection to our roots, our past, our community and, consequently, our present. She says, 'Living arts are an essential part of the social fabric of our communities, like planting seeds, reaping the fruits of our labors, and preserving our food. Such traditions are the backbone of what makes a community a home, and preserving them ensures that future generations can enjoy the same quality of life with the same attention to detail, function and beauty.'

Alabama Chanin is the perfect embodiment of slow design, using age-old techniques to create products that celebrate strong design principles for modern living. Honouring the rich cultural heritage of cotton production in Alabama, Chanin openly recognizes the sometimes-ugly history, but also celebrates the constant connection to the past and the fibre within the community.

Chanin sells her work online through the Alabama Chanin website as well as high-end retailers, and organizes events which revolve around workshops, storytelling and sharing in the quilt-making tradition.

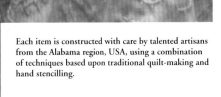

Each item is constructed with care by talented artisans from the Alabama region, USA, using a combination of techniques based upon traditional quilt-making and hand stencilling.

AMANA

Amana's philosophy is to create beautiful clothing using ethical production, and to illustrate that environmentally and socially responsible fashion can also equate to exquisite quality and design. Producing a sexy, wearable collection of dresses and coordinating separates with a sophisticated stylish edge and subtle colour stories, Amana sources all its fabrics from suppliers who manufacture with minimal impact on the environment. They aspire to consistently present collections that are not only desirable but also do not come at a cost to the environment. Amana means 'delivered in trust' in Arabic.

Produced in Ain Leuh, in the Middle Atlas mountains in Morocco, all of Amana's garments are made by female artisans in a long-term fair-trade partnership. They work only with fabric suppliers who guarantee safe working conditions and living wages for their employees. Voluntarily working with the International Fair Trade Association (IFAT) guidelines, Amana pays three times the minimum wage, makes advance payments and helps producers with training and assists them in acquiring machinery and technology to grow their businesses. To offset the carbon emissions from the transportation of the garments from Morocco, Amana donates to projects in developing countries that reduce carbon emissions. Proud of its eco-credentials, Amana offers 'a collection where the customer can trust that from the cotton farmers to the finishing stitches, every effort has been made to respect the people involved and the ecosystem'.

Helen Wood, the creative partner, designs the garments, makes the patterns and samples, sources the fabrics and trimmings, and manages and trains the Moroccan artisans. Managing partner Erin Tabrar oversees the day-to-day running of the business, production and marketing. Both Wood and Tabrar became interested in sustainable practices while studying at Central Saint Martins and the London College of Fashion respectively. →

Artisans in Ain Leuh, Morocco, construct all of Amana's garments on a fair trade basis (above).

Amana's philosophy is to create clothes that marry
beautiful design with ethical production practices.

All cotton used in the collection is certified organic, as well as fair trade, guaranteeing minimum working conditions for the farmers. Amana also works with hemp, a naturally eco-friendly fabric, which requires little or no pesticides or fertilizers to grow, and consumes much less water than cotton while producing three times as much fibre. Organic silk and peace silk augment the collection. Peace silk means that the silkworms are allowed to live their full life cycle before the cocoons are harvested. The silk is then farmed and woven in India, where Amana only works with vertically integrated suppliers who own their mills and can guarantee working conditions and wages. A small amount of recycled polyester is also used, where the polyester fibres are recycled and woven into new fabrics. Tencel rounds out Amana's range of fabrics; made from wood pulp, it has an environmentally friendly production process.

The collection is sold through Amana's website and other online retailers and in boutiques across the UK and Europe. It is also shown at the major ethical trade shows such as Estethica and Pure.

Organic-produced cotton, silks and hemp are combined to create Amana's environmentally and socially responsible collection.

EL NATURALISTA

An international shoe brand, El Naturalista makes comfortable, quirky, fashionable footwear, as well as bags, inspired by nature and people. A shoe company with a global perspective and created by a humanitarian team, it originated in La Rioja, Spain, an area with a long and well-respected shoemaking tradition. Inspired by dreams of a better world, El Naturalista insists that its suppliers, factories, agents and sales personnel must be committed to earth-friendly practices and adhere to its environmental policy. Constantly working to improve their eco-policies, El Naturalista employs the least harmful materials possible in the production of their shoes, using natural materials and dyes and avoiding polluting or toxic substances. Maximizing its use of biodegradable and recyclable materials, the company uses recycled polyurethane inner linings, leather free from chromium and recycled rubber soles. The shoes are packaged in 100 per cent recycled cardboard printed with water-based inks. The company also provides fair pay and compensation to all employees, promoting traditional means of production while supporting the use of appropriate new technologies.

Travel is fundamental to the design team, headed by Francisco Sota. They take inspiration for each collection from the people, culture, history and legends they encounter on their journeys. Movement is El Naturalista's reason to exist. They believe that human beings are the earth's most valuable resource, hence social responsibility is fundamental to their corporate philosophy. Seeking out indigenous communities looking for opportunities for growth, they participate in an act of mutual learning. In collaboration with NGO Pro-Peru, they have developed the Atauchi Project, establishing a home for disabled and abandoned children in Arequipa, Peru, that shelters and educates 113 needy children. They have contributed hundreds of thousands of euros to date.

The company states, 'whatever our race or culture, we all walk in search of happiness'. El Naturalista enjoys creating comfortable and attractive footwear that helps people move along the amazing journey of life. Their corporate symbol of a frog represents a land made fertile by water and the perpetual fight against stagnation. Reflecting their nonconformist character, they want to demonstrate to the world that it is possible to travel in a different direction, along a different road, while enjoying life. They explain: 'We make shoes for people who embrace life as they walk'.

In 2005, El Naturalista received the Corporate Solidarity Award from the Mayor of Pamplona for its work with ASPACE, a non-profit organization that supports Cerebral Palsy. Together, they developed a special employment centre for physically and mentally disabled people.

With 90 per cent of all its production destined for export, El Naturalista sells in 45 countries. The company's own stand-alone stores operate in Helsinki, California and Paris. They sell their shoes online and exhibit at major trade shows in Spain, Germany, Milan and the USA.

Using natural materials and dyes, El Naturalista shoes are made from natural oiled leather, rubber and with recycled inner liners and soles wherever possible, with many styles sewn by hand.

'We make shoes for people who embrace life as they walk.'

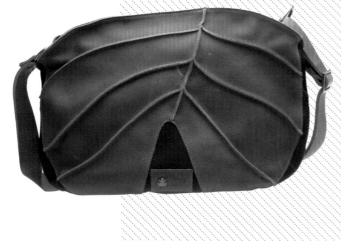

The quirky, earthly styling inherent in El Naturalista's designs is inspired by nature, and by the people and communities they have visited around the world.

ELENA GARCÍA

Born in Spain, Elena García has been based in London since 1992. She originally trained as a linguist, and her interpreting work with local groups raised awareness of the problems faced by migrant communities and people in prison. Deciding to explore her passion for design, García returned to school to study a degree in surface textiles for fashion at the London College of Fashion. She produced her first collection in collaboration with friend Ilya Fisher directly upon graduation.

García still works with Fisher and now also with Carolyn Abbott, both textile designers and friends who do the felting, cut work and specialized dyeing for the collections. Fisher is a shibori dye-resist artist, while Abbott is an experienced felt artist, trained by García and Fisher to make the jackets and camisoles for the collection.

Elena García's work blends daring design, traditional techniques and luxurious eco-friendly textiles to create beautiful timeless garments. The collection has a highly sophisticated aesthetic, with a vintage-like respect for couture processes and boudoir sensuality to it. It features silks made from organically fed silkworms and chemical-free processing. Much of the wool used in the collection for the nuno and needle felting comes from the organically reared British Bluefaced Leicester sheep. Details include special silver clasps and stunning shell buttons. All garments are handcrafted in the studio or produced by small local manufacturers and social enterprise units, working to provide employment for local women. Dyes are free of metal, amine and azo compounds, and promotional materials are printed on FSC-certified paper using vegetable inks. The brand works with local social enterprise units in Brick Lane, London, to do the embroidery and cut work. These groups also provide education, childcare and sewing skills to local women and work placements for women recently released from prison. García explains the company's philosophy: 'As creators, as designers, as business owners we have a responsibility to do what we can to preserve our world, so we source locally whenever possible, and we only use fabrics that are rapidly renewable and pesticide-free.'

The company also works with a Nepal-based manufacturing unit that shares García's passion for eco-fabrics and that works with 15 families and an extended network of hundreds of craftspeople in local villages to develop hemp and nettle knitwear for the label. They adhere to the e-credo of: organic, pesticide free, fair trade, local, ethical and sustainable.

A member of The Ethical Fashion Forum, the Eco Designers Network, the Conscious Designers Collective and the Centre for Sustainable Fashion, García is also the designer behind the upcycling label Sew Last Season, a hip menswear collection made from upcycled items to create limited-edition pieces. In addition, García works with Fisher on the design and manufacture of eco-clothing for London retailer Love Life Stories.

With coverage on style forecaster WGSN, as well as on Treehugger and in *Vogue* and *Selvedge* to name just a few, García's work has come to the notice of reporters like Suzy Menkes, who featured her work in an article. The collection is available online through the website, as well as through high-end boutiques across the UK and the USA.

An exquisite mix of organic silks and linen in indigo
and ivory, Elena García's collection is embellished with
felting, cut work, embroidery and shibori dyeing.

LEILA HAFZI

After meeting the amazing people of the Himalayas and seeing for herself how trade in Nepal had for centuries been locked between the two superpowers China and India, Leila Hafzi realized that the craftsmen and women of Nepal sorely needed guidance in product development to gear their products more towards the Western market. Working with tailors, hand knitters and craftspeople, Hafzi fell in love with the people and the place. It became her mission and passion to show the world what Nepal could do, working to develop small factories and acting like a window into the high-end luxury fashion industry. Traditional skilled Thanka painters form the basis of the craftspeople that hand paint Hafzi's exclusive designs. The cooperative that hand paints the silk, and with whom she works, is the only one in Nepal and was originally developed by a Dutch monk who brought Italian silk painters to train the Nepalese painters over 25 years ago. Hafzi elaborates: 'Realizing the effect of product development in the Third World made me passionate about the work, proving that ethical and ecological trade is possible in high-end fashion.'

Hafzi has built a network across Nepal and now works with the best fabrics and tailors the country has to offer. Her goal of introducing an ecological and ethical global trading company in Nepal has remained unchanged since she first established her label. She is working towards the development of an entirely environmentally friendly production cycle, as she explains, 'for me, it is a balance between creating works in developing countries, establishing a long-term market position and then step by step making fully ecological collections'. Every piece in the collection is produced in Nepal, mostly from imported geige Chinese and Indian silk, and hand painted or dyed in Nepal, using low-impact dyes and a closed-circuit water management system. Hafzi also creates a collection of refined chic daywear pieces from Eco-Tex-certified pashmina yarns and long lacy dresses finely knitted from nettle fibre, which is →

Working with traditional Thanka painters (left) in Katmandu, Nepal, Leila Hafzi creates exquisite hand-painted, as well as draped, silk gowns.

sourced from Mongolia but knitted in Nepal. Ethical production, nevertheless, faces many challenges in Nepal, with limited access to eco-friendly fabrics, as well as technical and production restrictions.

Some of Leila Hafzi's more lavish red-carpet gowns use as much as 25 metres of silk and take four artists up to four days to hand paint. Her sophisticated and elegant gowns have complex and extravagant draping, reminiscent of Grecian and Egyptian styles in their grandeur and impact. They are inspired by Tibetan monks' cloaks, mixed with equal measure of 1970s glam and Greek goddess. Her intricately hand-painted floral garlands, peacock feathers and exotic animals in vibrant jewel tones are her signature and embellish her extravagant and voluminous gowns with their strategic placement. Her shorter cocktail-length dresses are no less luxurious, with fine hand-dyed silk chiffon and voluminous silhouettes. Hafzi also produces a knitwear collection of sophisticated daywear with understated wearable pieces in subtle ombré dyes, and a small crystal jewellery collection that is tailor-made to complement her clothing line.

Leila Hafzi was the first Norwegian designer ever to create clothing for the French catalogue company La Redoute. She now sells her own collection through high-end boutiques across the Middle East and Europe, with her signature pieces often seen adorning celebrities at red-carpet events.

The elegant hand painting, dyeing and draping of the
silk garments engages multiple artisans for several days
to achieve the precision and care inherent in each and
every piece.

LES FÉES DE BENGALE

Les Fées de Bengale's website says it all. Opening with 'Once upon a time', a Maple tree seed cursor and hearts floating up from a ground of poppy flowers, it sets the scene for a collection full of fantasy and fairytales. The website tells the story of three young women from Paris with the same philosophy – 'My vice is dreaming' – and a common vision: to create a label for women by women, while respecting the planet and each individual that plays a role in the production of the collection. Their work is fashionable, ethical and organic, and entirely made from ecological and natural fibres, including jersey, drop needle rib and baby fleece, all made from organic cotton. Organic cotton satin and cotton voile inject whimsy and femininity to the collection, while organic cotton twill adds an urban edge. The collection consists of pretty feminine separates and dresses. Items are floaty and flounced, with generous cuts, clever tucking details and playful silhouettes. It offers an urban angel look with a casual *Sex in the City* flavour, only set in Paris instead of New York, and featuring off-the-shoulder angel-wing T-shirts worn over wide-leg trousers. Colours include petal, cappuccino, storm, sand and oriental blue, adding a touch of retro glamour to the look. The designers intend to bring 'a touch of femininity in fair trade, as well as a touch of humanity in fashion'.

Having travelled around India in search of suppliers that displayed a desire to develop capacity and competency, as well as a willingness to work with and support destitute women through social projects, Les Fées de Bengale selected an NGO that manages 30 small cooperatives in the slums of Mumbai (formerly Bombay). Each cooperative consists of about 20 women, each one of whom receives six months of general sewing training and an additional two years of coaching and training in the sewing workshop. Various support systems are in place to assist the women with their transition from the street. Micro-loan programmes are available to support the creation of new sewing workshops, to purchase new equipment, to pursue other professional activities and to improve their children's education. The project is funded by profits, with 30 to 40 per cent of the NGO's profits used to develop new activities and programmes. The partners, Elodie le Derf, Camille Dupuy and Sophie Dupuy, travel to India twice a year to work directly with the women in the cooperative, teaching them dressmaking and sewing techniques.

The collection is sold through Les Fées de Bengale's own website and other online resources, as well as in boutiques across France, the UK, Switzerland and Germany. They have received press coverage in *Marie Claire*, *Elle* and French *Vogue*.

Organic cotton jersey, baby fleece, voile, twill, silk and lace are fashioned into youthful, romantic, playful and urban styles by Les Fées de Bengale.

MODAFUSION

ModaFusion is a collective of graduates from Paris's Institut Français de la Mode (IFM) that work with cooperatives and NGOs in Rio de Janeiro, Brazil, to produce ethical collections, conduct workshops and instigate collective collaborations through artistic fusion. Focusing on fashion, design, photography and music, ModaFusion forms a creative laboratory, joining Brazilian and French artists and working exclusively with Lente dos Sonhos models, a model agency situated in the city's 'Cidade de Deus' ('City of God') neighbourhood and founded by photographer Tony Barros. In 2005, Brazilian artisans and IFM graduates collaborated in the year of Brazil in France. ModaFusion is now working towards the year of France in Brazil, creating opportunities for both countries to extend their cultural and economic ties. The collective explains, 'Our objective is to help [disfavoured communities] to develop artistically and transform their artisans' savoir faire into fashion products.'

AndreaFusion is one such fashion collaboration, produced in conjunction with Andrea Crews and several Brazilian cooperatives and selling in Colette in Paris. ModaFusion has also produced a collection of clothing made entirely from bamboo fibre and a lingerie collection in collaboration with Daspu, a collective of Brazilian prostitutes that was already selling a highly popular line of T-shirts across Brazil.

Each year, three collections are produced. One of these always focuses on a specific social cause and joins a particular Brazilian NGO with a renowned French designer. The first such collaboration in 2007 was between Daspu and Fifi Chachnil, a French designer who has designed lingerie for Madonna. The name Daspu is a play on words, using 'pu', short for 'puta', meaning 'whore' in Portuguese, and 'Daslu', an exclusive high-end boutique in São Paulo. Daspu showed the collection during Rio Fashion Week, modelled by the prostitutes themselves, in a venue known as a place to ply their trade. The collaboration between Daspu and Fifi Chachnil has been exhibited at the Prêt-à-Porter Show and the Ethical Fashion Show in Paris. →

ModaFusion's purpose is to create ethical, cultural and economic opportunities in Brazil, based on fair commerce principles. Many designs incorporate traditional Brazilian artisanal techniques such as fuxico, crochet, silk painting and embroidery.

The second annual collection, made in collaboration with Crocheteira da Maré, Vida Real, Coosturart and Ieda Campos, a group of four cooperatives working with various different techniques including crochet, silk painting, embroidery and local techniques such as fuxico, is known collectively as 'Anjos da Favela' ('Angels from the Slum'). Each year, one IFM alumni spends three months in Rio, working with the cooperative or cooperatives of their choice, to produce a collection through the ModaFusion label. The collective aims 'to promote the idea that future creation lies in disfavoured communities. The slum's genuine creativity constitutes a strong identity for Brazilian fashion and a source of uncommon inspiration for Western fashion.'

A third collection is based upon the work produced by artisans taught at ModaFusion workshops over a period of three to six months. ModaFusion is supported by Western companies that wish to work with and invest in Brazilian artisanal work.

The ModaFusion line can be bought at high-end boutiques and department stores across Paris, including Le Bon Marché, L'Eclaireur and Colette, with a special collection available at cut-price retailers Monoprix.

MONA MOHANNA

Mona Mohanna was born in Lebanon in 1970. Moving to Italy in 1989, she attended the prestigious Reggio Emilia school in Calabria to pursue her education in fashion planning and production. At the International Handicraft Fair in Florence in 1999, she presented her first collection of linen dresses entitled 'Controlled Seduction', which explored the relationship between Muslim women and seduction. The dresses were embroidered by Palestinian refugees in the Sidon and Tyre refugee camps. Mohanna says, 'My designs pull upon multiple traditions. I use Palestinian embroidery and Arab traditional textiles and beads.'

The 2009 collection includes a wide range of kaftans, robes, jackets and coats, richly embellished with traditionally inspired embroideries, woven from Pakistani linen, silk and cotton, and produced in a dizzying array of colours. Many of the materials are sourced in Syria, including the local hand-loomed silk and the recycled glass beads. Traditional designs are reinterpreted for modern Western needs, with styles such as the man's *abaya*, a short robe, reworked for the female form and made from the finest wool gauze. Long flowing kaftans skim the body in silk shantung or rich jewel-toned silk seersucker. Jackets in shimmering and subtle shades are adorned with rich embroidery in every conceivable design, or entirely hand pick-stitched and quilted. Designs are floral and geometric, reminiscent of rich Persian carpets in their bold use of colour and pattern. Mohanna also produces a wide range of shawls, wraps and scarves, knotted, twisted, beaded and embroidered to complement her collections, and a jewellery line strung on silk cords or quilted and padded for effect.

The philosophy behind Mona Mohanna's collection is the fusion of Western and Arab cultures, as she explains: 'I tried to apply the Western cuts on traditional embroidery and textiles to better fit the needs of my target audience.' The fundamental characteristic of her work is her ability to harmonize the traditional techniques and materials of the Middle East with the needs and preferences of women from the Western world. Her designs leave enough room for the talented Arabic embroiderers to freely express themselves through their work as well as to develop and stretch their skills. Guaranteeing fair pay and good working conditions, Mohanna encourages women from the Palestinian refugee camps to be creative, while mostly working from home to allow them to spend time with their families. The motivation behind establishing the label came with the end of the war in Lebanon when so many young Lebanese were leaving the country; Mohanna wanted to share her own experiences and skills with her fellow citizens to persuade them to stay in Lebanon.

The line has a base range of popular styles that remain constant, with colours and fabrics changing seasonally and new designs supplementing the original pieces each season. Mona Mohanna's collection of clothing, shawls, scarves, bags and jewellery sells across Italy.

The main characteristic of Mona Mohanna's work is the harmony she creates through the use of traditional Middle Eastern techniques and materials, such as hand-loomed Syrian textiles, and a Western interpretation of style and form.

NOIR

One of the collections spearheading a marked departure from the marginalized market that spawned it is Noir by Danish designer Peter Ingwersen. It is a super-chic luxury fashion label that benefits the people of Third World countries through trade rather than aid, by creating 'meaningful consumption'.

Noir produces clothing and accessories made under fair working conditions. Illuminati II, the textile arm of the company, supplies sub-Saharan fair trade organic cotton fabrics to Noir and other fashion brands. They worked directly with Ugandan farmers to develop long-staple organic cotton. Fabrics are also sourced from European mills and ethical textile resources in China and India. Between 60 and 80 per cent of the textiles used in the collection are made from organic cotton or other ethically produced fibres. The company adheres to the ten principles of the United Nations Global Compact, as well as the UN's Universal Declaration of Human Rights, the International Labour Organization Conventions and the International Chamber of Commerce's Business Charter for Sustainable Development, and is reviving an industry in Uganda that brings money back into the community. Noir has chosen to distance itself, however, from other sustainable labels, preferring to be judged on its design skill and taste, rather than its sustainable practices. This choice is a marked departure from most other labels, where practice comes first and design second. Noir is clearly stating that it is not afraid to be judged against the best that fashion has to offer. Ingwersen explains, 'I totally respect what everyone is doing for ethical clothing, but at the same time I don't want to be lumped as "that ethical clothes label". Our garments look like normal stylish clothes, made from luxurious fabrics and, unless you knew about us, you'd never guess the organic provenance.'

The collection is the antithesis of hippy, and is in fact, utterly refined. Noir's signature look incorporates hard-edged tailoring with dark sexual undertones. According to Ingwersen, consumers buy Noir because they are attracted to the pure designs and because they know that some corporate responsibility is associated with it: 'First, it's the most beautiful collection and, second, it has the finest cotton in the world, and it may justify people's spending, knowing that a certain amount will go back to the people who helped pick the cotton.'

Noir sells to a dizzying array of high-end and luxury boutiques around the globe, from the UK to Russia and including Belgium, Egypt, Turkey, Australia and the Faroe Islands, to mention just a few.

The raison d'être is to show that sexiness, luxury, fashion and corporate social responsibility can work beautifully together in both the Noir and Black Noir collections.

Certified organic and fair trade cotton grown in
Uganda forms the basis of the Noir collection.

ROYAH

An ethical design company from Afghanistan, Royah brings together art and development for women. A vehicle through which to present the rich Afghan cultural heritage, Royah was set up in Kabul in 2005 with a handful of women who wanted to make a difference. Drawing on Afghanistan's rich artistic legacy, Royah creates contemporary fashions using Afghan textiles combined with Italian expertise. Working with local artisans, using mostly traditional hand-loomed fabrics and incorporating the magnificent geometric embroideries made famous by Pashtun women, Royah produces traditional and innovative reinterpretations of Afghan fabrics. Employing 20 women in Kabul, the company supports women's rights in a place where access to work and freedom of expression have been denied. Gabriella Ghidoni, the founder of Royah, explains, 'It is essential to train and support the women who lost so much during 23 years of war.'

Historically, Afghanistan was part of the silk route, forming the link between East and West. The country's silk, once lauded as among the finest in the world, has been one of the many casualties of the war; Afghanistan has been robbed of its industry and ancient and intricate embroidery patterns are now lost. Royah employs skilled Afghan artisans to reclaim these ancient handicrafts using local fabrics: precious hand-loomed silks from Herat, cotton Ikat, Chitrali wool and those featuring tribal embroidery patterns. Collections are the result of the continuous search for and development of antique Persian and Islamic patterns, reinterpreted in a transcultural and creative manner.

Ghidoni is dedicated to promoting and growing ethical fashion. Working in developing countries, she trains vulnerable groups in clothing design and production. She believes in the value of ethical trading and is committed to sharing her experience as a professional with women in Afghanistan. Graduating from the University of Padua in Italy with a degree in psychology, Ghidoni focused on understanding the real needs of vulnerable people in developing countries. Honing her psychological skills by providing counselling relief to child soldiers in Sierra Leone, Ghidoni bases her work on strengthening capacity where there is potential.

Ghidoni has lived in Afghanistan since 2003. Working as a stress counsellor for the United Nations for the first year, she then established Royah. In Farsi, 'Royah' means 'the woman who has a vision, the dreamer'. For Ghidoni, this vision is to enable Afghan women to earn an income and improve their lives. She is also a consultant for the International Labour Organization, Terre Solidali and DACAAR (a Danish NGO working with Afghan refugees in Pakistan and Afghanistan, training them in design and fashion). Using her skills as a fashion designer, she has trained 40 women in Kabul in fashion and jewellery design. Her students have gone on to open their own association, working as a profit-making enterprise.

Available to purchase in high-end boutiques in Italy and through the atelier in Afghanistan, Ghidoni's work has also been published in Italian and British magazines.

Bringing together art and development for women, Royah draws on Afghanistan's rich cultural heritage to create contemporary fashions by reinterpreting designs and details from ancient Islamic and Persian patterns.

SENSE-ORGANICS

sense-organics manufactures and distributes a full line of women's, men's and children's sportswear made from organic cotton and blends of environmentally friendly fibres. Based in Germany, Kirsten Weihe-Keidel founded the company in 1997. The women's collection, under the label So Pure, is wearable and casually stylish, featuring pretty jersey tops and printed T-shirts alongside jackets and colourful accessories. When Kirsten first started the company, she focused on product and technical development in the narrow market of childrenswear, choosing to build her expertise in a niche market before expanding into womenswear and then lingerie. sense-organics also decided to keep its profit margin lower than average, 'so that anyone with a conscience can afford one of our GOTS [Global Organic Textile Standard] certified, organic cotton T-shirts if they want'.

Responsible for every aspect of manufacturing – from growing the cotton, spinning the thread and making the fabrics, to the low-impact dyeing processes and employment practices – sense-organics has been producing organic cotton clothing through non-profit employment programmes in the Tamil Nadu region in India since 1997. Working with two fair trade projects in India, which they helped to organize and which they support through profits, they pioneered the use of organic and pesticide-free cotton in India. Zameen, one of sense-organics fair trade partners, focuses on improving the livelihoods of rural farming communities by ensuring that farmers receive better prices for their products through fair trade and organic certification. Farmers are actively encouraged to shift from conventional cotton production to organic cultivation by being guaranteed their income through having their cotton bought. →

sense-organics is responsible for every aspect of manufacturing, from growing the cotton, spinning the thread, and making the fabrics, to low-impact dyeing processes and ethical employment practices.

The fair trade cotton DAA collection consists of celebrity designed T-shirts, hoodies, underwear and nightwear for men and women.

sense-organics also produces a collection under the Designers Against Aids (DAA) label (see page 176), which is provocative and tongue-in-cheek, with in-your-face, to-the-point graphic messages on the topic of safe sex. Founded in 2004 by the non-profit organization Beauty Without Irony, DAA raises awareness among young people about AIDS. sense-organics works with multiple designers, musicians and celebrities to produce items made of organic cotton under fair trade conditions in India. The long-standing collaboration with DAA has sense-organics supplying the T-shirt blanks, having already perfected the fabric, fit and style, with the celebrities designing the prints. They make no profit from their part in the collaboration, simply covering their production costs. The T-shirts sell at H&M and a quarter of sales are donated to HIV/AIDS prevention projects around the world. Artists collaborating on this project include Rihanna, Chicks on Speed, Good Charlotte, Jade Jagger, Katharine Hamnett and Timberland.

Weihe-Keidel's next focus is to develop a men's and women's wool suit collection, which she is looking at producing in the traditional home of high-quality tailoring: Italy. With so much focus on development in Third World countries and communities, people have forgotten that many industries closer to home are dying or languishing, with generations of small family businesses biting the dust in the face of the global economic meltdown and the exportation of production. Weihe-Keidel thinks it most appropriate to produce suits in Italy and to support local tailors and textile producers.

While the DAA T-shirts sell exclusively to H&M, the So Pure collection sells in boutiques around the world, including Belgium, France, Japan, Taiwan and Canada.

SHOTO
BANERJI

Trained as a textile designer, first in India, then at Central Saint Martins in London, Shoto Banerji has always been fascinated by the connection between the material and the finished garment. Her graduating collection combined ceramics, knitwear and jewellery, and had to be fired in the kiln at 1200°C.

Since 1999, Banerji has worked with traditional hand-loom weavers in central India, producing a collection of shawls, stoles and scarves in silk and in blends of wool and silk that are based on the artisans' cotton-sari-weaving skills. Her production helps to conserve the traditional weaving skills of these artisans while broadening their skills in a wider range of fabrics and products better suited to the international market. She explains: 'India is a vast country with a rich history of hand-loom weaving, which like most artisanal skills needs support to survive in the present times.' Banerji presents a unique range of inspirational fabrics in which the link between inspiration and product is part of the finished piece.

Diverse in character, hand-loom weaving is influenced by the culture, architecture and features particular to a region, with each region developing its own directory of design that sets it apart. The Maheshwari school of weavers that Banerji works with were originally Hindu and Muslim weavers commissioned for their skills in weaving saris and elaborate turbans. In the late eighteenth century, they combined their talents to design saris for the newly widowed queen of Indore, Rajmata Ahilyadevi Holkar, who could not be seen to wear anything flamboyant. Tasteful geometric borders heightened the elegance of her cotton mourning saris and have endured as a popular pattern today. Banerji elaborates: 'My work has been closely linked with the hand-loom weavers of Maheshwar in central India. The purpose has been to try and blend the weavers' age-old skills with the demands of the more modern marketplace, and to try and see if they could transcend their traditional home markets to ones overseas.'

The end product is luxurious to the touch, comfortable to wear, visually striking and represents understated elegance. Silk and occasionally linen act as the base for Banerji's designs, and certain carefully selected grades of wool add warmth. Birds, orchids and the traditional pattern of the weavers have inspired collections. The varied forms and tones of these influences inform each collection's colour palette, while the elaborate dyeing process mimics the complexity of nature itself. Yarns are carefully selected and sourced from Australia, Belgium, Italy, India and Thailand. Due to the amount of time spent in research and development, Banerji prefers to sell her pieces in context, planning gallery-type exhibitions that showcase photographic studies alongside the actual shawls, and has organized such events in the USA and in Germany. She has also exhibited her works in Mumbai, Delhi, Singapore, Brussels, London and Antwerp.

Shoto Banerji produces a unique range of inspirational, hand-loomed fabrics fashioned into a collection of shawls, stoles and scarves.

TALLER FLORA

Founded by Carla Fernandez, Taller Flora is a fashion label and mobile laboratory that travels throughout Mexico visiting indigenous communities that create handmade textiles and garments. With a growing base of artisans, Taller Flora is an innovative business model with its own fair trade network and set of environmental policies to foster responsible practices in fashion. Having developed methodology for artisans to communicate through their craft, Fernandez believes that tradition is not static and fashion is not ephemeral. She thinks that 'only radical contemporary design will prevent the extinction of craftsmanship'.

Born on the northern border of Mexico close to Texas, Fernandez inherited from her mother the habit of shopping at malls and Salvation Army stores across the border. Her father, the director of the National Institute of Anthropology and History, travelled all over Mexico with Carla, who would spend hours looking at local clothing, trying to find traditional items to incorporate into her own wardrobe. Standing out in school because of how she dressed, Fernandez continued to experiment by mixing traditional Mexican clothing with Western pieces.

Studying garment construction at an indigenous textile and clothing museum, Fernandez realized that almost all traditional pieces were made exclusively of squares or rectangles, a form of construction diametrically opposed to her fashion-school education. Ancient Mexican patterning has an elaborate system of pleats, folds and seams to construct a vast array of garments using only squares and rectangles; with its own system of assembly, it is a kind of 'cloth origami'. Connecting her interest for geometric clothing construction with her studies in fashion design and art history, Fernandez soon realized her dream of working with indigenous communities when she was asked by the Institute of Folk Cultures to teach dressmaking at a travelling craft-design school. →

Working with indigenous Mexican communities, Taller Flora builds on the complex system of pleats, folds and seams in traditional garments to produce a radically contemporary collection.

'Only radical contemporary design will prevent the extinction of craftsmanship.'

Designs reinterpret the traditional Mexican system of using only squares and rectangles into contemporary, conceptual, modern garments.

Every two months, Fernandez visits different indigenous communities to study the way they make clothes. On each trip, she makes new discoveries about the square geometry of traditional dressmaking patterns. These patterns are copied and catalogued to create a compendium of formal solutions that are valuable to all designers. At the same time, Fernandez develops items for her own collection in collaboration with the artisanal groups. One of her missions is to enhance artisanal creativity based on their own methods and by using processes that are familiar to them. This also helps to establish ties with different cooperatives and to strengthen fair trade networks that use environmentally friendly materials.

Garments combining craft processes with the Taller Flora workshop's in-house designs form part of the haute couture collection, while her prêt-à-porter line features industrial processes and materials with only some handcrafted details. This allows Fernandez to produce enough garments to supply stores, while offering a more extensive line of clothing and ensuring that the cooperatives she collaborates with have constant work.

The winner of the British Council's International Young Fashion Entrepreneur Award in 2008, to develop two new collections in cooperation with Mexico's largest producer, Fernandez continues to expand the ways in which she interprets indigenous design. The judges stated: 'She has a clear and distinct design philosophy, which is highly personal and representative of her cultural identity, while speaking to the international fashion industry.'

VAN MARKOVIEC

Founded in 2005 by fashion designer Kasia Markowska and environmental scientist Zuzia Andziak, Van Markoviec is inspired by the slow fashion movement. The two partners have complementary skills but entirely different educational backgrounds, and share the same sensitivity to creation. The fashionista meets environmentalist label follows the 'seven Rs': Respect for people's rights with acceptable working conditions; Reduced use of unsustainable natural resources and a reduction in emissions and overproduction; Reuse; Remanufacture and Recycle waste; Rethink production life cycles; and Redesign. Aiming to create a synergy between luxurious design and an eco-philosophy, Van Markoviec transforms the finest environmentally friendly fabrics into contemporary fashions through ecologically sound production and according to fair trade principles. The duo strives to design from a wide-ranging perspective while crafting a fashionable and sustainable collection, under the motto 'Quality is luxury'.

Determined to take responsibility for garment production, Van Markoviec contributes to the reduction of carbon dioxide emissions by shortening its sampling chain, producing locally, minimizing waste and reusing and recycling leftovers. The label only uses eco-certified textiles with natural and nickel-free metal trimmings. A commitment to transparency in manufacturing forms the foundation for the entire company, with a focus on researching and incorporating innovative new materials into the design process. The collection features organic cotton and organic cotton blended with silk and linen, all JOCA-certified (the Japan Organic Cotton Association) for social and environmental production methodology through the entire life cycle. Van Markoviec also uses hemp and hemp blends, natural silk dyed with GOTS-certified plant pigments and catfish skins, a leftover from the fish industry that also supports fair employment. Natural materials are used to make unique accessories and jewellery items, all sourced from renewable natural resources such as their own textile waste. All producers and manufacturers comply with the International Labour Organization (ILO) and the Declaration of Human Rights.

Closely collaborating with research institutions in an effort to bring innovative new textiles to their collection, Markowska and Andziak helped to start the 'green fashion project' with The Cartesius Institute in the Netherlands. Their aim is to set up a network of designers, experts, producers, developers and NGOs working in green fashion.

Markowska and Andziak's long-term goal is to continue to expand their brand recognition while remaining exclusive. They would like to be known equally for their contemporary design, sustainable manufacturing and fair trade principles.

Sold through their own store in Arnhem, the Netherlands, Van Markoviec is also available online and at wholesale. The brand participates in many international trade and fashion shows in Copenhagen, New York, Tokyo, Berlin and Los Angeles.

The Van Markoviec collection aspires to assuage the aesthete as well as the conscience by combining organic textiles, fair trade production and contemporary design.

Transforming the finest environmentally friendly materials into contemporary fashions under fair trade principles, Van Markoviec uses 100 per cent natural silk and hemp, organic cotton and linen dyed with plant pigments.

Chapter Two

ECOLOGICAL & SLOW DESIGN

The growth of the ecological fashion fabric industry has finally reached a state where designers do not feel unduly restricted in their fabric choices. Textiles like hemp, previously coarse and roughly woven, have long been combined with silk, bamboo and other fibres in the weaving process to produce refined and varied fabrics for multiple markets, including high-end fashion design. The development of new fibres such as soy, milk, bamboo, seaweed and nettle has added to the diversity, texture and expression of ecological materials available to designers. Fair trade and community support, as well as other ethical production methods – such as azo-free dyeing, water-filtration systems for the recycling of water used in the dyeing process and the use of traditional vegetable dyes – have made ethical textiles available in more than just boring beige. Rather a plethora of textures, shades and finishes allow designers to satisfy their conscience while expressing their creativity with minimal restriction. Various ethical and ecological standardization bodies have helped in the formation and evaluation of the required standards for growing and producing natural and synthetic fibres and textiles. There is still some way to go in the standardization of accreditation bodies across a range of textiles and production methods, with terms like 'ecological' and 'natural' relatively open to interpretation; nevertheless, it is much clearer and more defined than previously.

The history of ecological and organic manufacture has its roots in multiple ranges of undyed beige T-shirts with political and socially aware slogans, developed mostly by activists not aesthetes. Although this area of design still has a valid place and market, it is not now thankfully the only expression of the use of ecological fabrication. Designers who use only ethical and sustainable production methods that bring no harm to the environment can now stand against the best that fashion design has to offer. The commitment of some designers has to be admired. Linda Loudermilk in the USA, for example, has stuck it out while fabrics were developed and ranges broadened; others, such as Laura Strambi of Yoj, have themselves aided in the advancement of the textiles or dyeing techniques.

Slow design, or a return to traditional craft techniques and practices, rounds out this chapter with wonderful examples of designers who adhere to age-old traditions of handcrafted skills and/or combine those traditions with all that the technological age has to offer their craft. Designers such as Christine Birkle for HUT UP and Françoise Hoffmann employ the technique of felting, with its ancient history and multiple cultural expressions, but nevertheless combine it with high-tech printing and graphic techniques or simply very modern design concepts to bring the craft back to life and imbue it with a currency not valid for centuries. Other designers, such as Samant Chauhan, help to sustain and value culturally specific and centuries-old traditions of hand weaving by working directly with artisanal weavers and incorporating their work into beautifully conceived collections.

Camilla Norrback produces an eco luxury collection that incorporates ecological cotton, alpaca, luxurious cashmere and silk.

ALEXANDRA FARO

Alexandra Faro grew up in Budapest, Hungary. After years of travelling through Europe and several wild years in Tokyo, she moved to London to continue her education, studying design at the London College of Fashion and fine art and painting at Kensington and Chelsea College. Faro gained experience working for the lingerie label St Tropez and participated in Judy Blame's Cruise Collection for Louis Vuitton and Swarovski's Runway Rocks. She had been working in the fashion industry for approximately five years prior to starting her own collection in 2008. Consistently inspired by paintings and installations by contemporary female artists such as Marlene Dumas and Louise Bourgeois, Faro tends towards themes and concepts that revolve around issues like women's power struggle in post-modern society and their constant search for identity.

The Alexandra Faro collection has a feminine, soft and intriguing style with clean silhouettes and understated colourways, yet integrates vibrant dashes of colour and print in surprising ways. Using sculptural and architectural lines and working mostly with solid colour, Faro achieves an interplay of texture and drape. Coming from a fine-art background, she designs like a painter, with large sweeping brushstrokes, adoring and exploring the mistakes that inevitably happen along the way – a fine artist's sensibility, not a fashion designer's. Faro creates voluminous dresses with a strong sense of direction and a tendency towards large blocks of colour; her first collection was entirely in black. For Faro, colour evokes feelings and emotion: 'I like to offer liberating, fun, out-of-the-ordinary clothes to my clients, so they can feel distant from social criticism and be themselves.'

Faro is looking for a way to combine sustainability and high fashion and to draw attention to the moral aspects of the fashion industry. Despite being a new and independent label, the collection is self supporting, an amazing achievement for a young fashion label.

Working mostly with silk, and peace silk wherever possible, Faro also uses fair trade Scottish wool and is experimenting with natural vegetable dyes. She also works to minimize waste through the production process and recycles everything possible. Faro occasionally works with recycled garments, with one such piece made entirely of recycled doll's clothes to draw attention to garment workers' rights and the West's throwaway culture.

Participating in the international trade shows Prêt-à-Porter, Atmosphere and Pure, Alexandra Faro sells through a store in Brick Lane, London, as well as in Zurich and through her own website, and has built a private client base that includes Zara Martin.

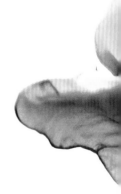

Solid colours in peace silk and fair trade wool form the base fabric for natural vegetable dye experimentation in Alexandra Faro's work.

'I like to offer liberating, fun, out-of-the-ordinary clothes to my clients, so they can feel distant from social criticism and be themselves.'

Inspired by the paintings and installations of contemporary female artists, Alexandra Faro's designs are structured as architectural silhouettes.

CAMILLA NORRBACK

Sharp tailored shapes and straight-edged flowing forms, monochromatic colourways and subtle patterning come together in Camilla Norrback's modern luxury line. Smoky and seductive, it is also chemical-free and made from environmentally certified natural fabrics. Using vegetable-dyed silk, naturally colour-grown cotton and indigo- and tannin-dyed fabrics, Norrback fashions collections inspired by 1930s American working-class sensibilities and Andrew Wyeth paintings from the mid-1940s. Wyeth's hyperrealism and subdued colours influence the subtle but emotionally symbolic coloration of the collection, which features cream, black and faded pastels. Specializing in new and innovative materials, Norrback puts great emphasis on finding new fabrics and new ways of working with them, especially through the dyeing process.

Norrback states, 'Modern luxury is as much about the inside as it is about the outside, giving yourself that which is good for both body and conscience.' In contrast to the throwaway mentality, she only uses ecological fabrics that are environmentally sound from cultivation through to processing and colouring. Impacting the environment as little as possible, pigments are not released into the groundwater, so the finishing contains no toxins or heavy metals that could be harmful to the wearer or the environment. 'The chemical-focused textile industry of today not only expends the environment, it also creates garments that are in fact harmful to the wearer's skin and contributes to an outdated and unsustainable society.'

With the growth of the ecological movement, environment-friendly technology for fabric production has evolved enough to allow an ethically minded designer complete artistic freedom. Categorizing her collection as 'eco-luxury', Norrback takes the utmost pride in producing collections that combine luxurious materials with exceptional quality and design. Expanding her use of fabrics to include recycled polyester and naturally tanned leather, Norrback creates a collection that embodies modern femininity, encompassing separates, dresses and lightweight knits. She explains: 'A garment of the highest quality that is justly manufactured [allows] the wearer to feel both beautiful and proud.'

Building the company from scratch and wholly self-financed, Norrback now sells the line in about 50 independent retailers around the globe, including her own concept store in Stockholm. Norrback has also worked in collaboration with Topshop's pop-up store in London, called Edit, where international designers were selected to sell their collection during a time-limited campaign. Each season, the collection is shown in Stockholm as well as at trade shows in Copenhagen, Paris and Berlin. Norrback has agents in France, the USA, the Netherlands and South Korea and has had a wide range of press coverage from *Teen Vogue* to *Elle* France and *The Guardian* newspaper in the UK.

Ecological and environmentally certified natural materials form the basis for Camilla Norrback's film noir aesthetic.

Silk dyed with madder berries, naturally colour-grown cotton, and tannin- and indigo-dyed cotton reflect the painterly inspiration and subdued tones of the Norrback collection.

CÉLINE FAIZANT

Graduating from the Union Chamber sewing school in Paris, Céline Faizant worked as a first hand and modeller in some of the most renowned ateliers of Paris, including Chanel Haute Couture and Christian Lacroix. Her atypical career started on the French Riviera, where she sold her own creations in the craft markets of Saint-Tropez and Saint Raphaël. In artist squats in Paris, she conducted experimental work in recycling fabric created from plastic and industrial materials, producing a line of 'resurrected' clothing. Her work took on an additional dimension when she combined her creativity with her commitment to the protection of the planet, motivated by a four-year survey of textile-industry pollution.

Developing her own techniques that are neither haute couture nor ready-to-wear, Faizant creates collections that feature a lot of hand stitching. Styles are edgy and conceptual, with unusual silhouettes and proportions and intriguing detailing and draping. Each collection comprises of a limited number of pieces realized in ecological, organic or fair trade fabrics, using only natural fibres from biological or biodynamic agriculture, with no genetically modified crop content, pesticides or chemical fertilizers. The growers adhere to the principles of fallow soil and crop rotation. All hemp and wool are ECOCERT-certified, with cotton and linen carrying the SKAL or ECOCERT label. Faizant also works with a few small manufacturers and cooperatives that lack the technical or financial means to afford organic certification, but that are, nevertheless, substantially complying with its standards. As she explains: 'If it is difficult for poor countries to develop their equipment, it is as difficult for rich countries to maintain it.' →

Developing her own techniques, which are neither haute couture nor ready-to-wear, Céline Faizant's collection is individually adjusted and fitted on the model, and finished by hand.

All garments are manufactured in fabrics that respect the planet and its inhabitants and are biodegradable. Synthetic fibres such as polyester, polyamide and elastane, all of which are produced from limited petrol reserves, are excluded from the collections. Faizant states, 'Our first ecological criteria is to offer natural raw materials – linen, hemp, cotton, wool or silk – and to exclude any synthetic fibres.'

To allow customers to evaluate each garment, an 'identity card' tag is attached to each item, detailing the fabric's origin, its production and processes. Céline Faizant clothing is produced in France, mostly by employee-bought-out companies. In all the channels of distribution, the brand endeavours to work with companies in which the employees share in the profit or are shareholders or owners of the business. For Faizant, fair trade does not mean delocalization, rather it is about enhancing local know-how instead. The label also works with artisanal cooperatives in Mali that produce beautiful handwoven and handcrafted weaves. Cotton comes from local producers and is cultivated according to ancestral methods. Even the packaging of the garments adheres to ecological standards, with each piece coming in an unbleached or undyed canvas bag made from SKAL-certified organic cotton, designed to be used again and again. For Faizant, it is imperative to 'allow a responsible consumption by offering transparency in manufacturing networks'.

The Céline Faizant collections sell in Paris, Biarritz, Bordeaux and Switzerland and are available online.

The collection promotes the use of craft techniques and reflects local culture, with craftsmen and artists creating original fabrics and accessories, such as the Mali-created handwoven bogolan and colour-woven kente cloth (far right).

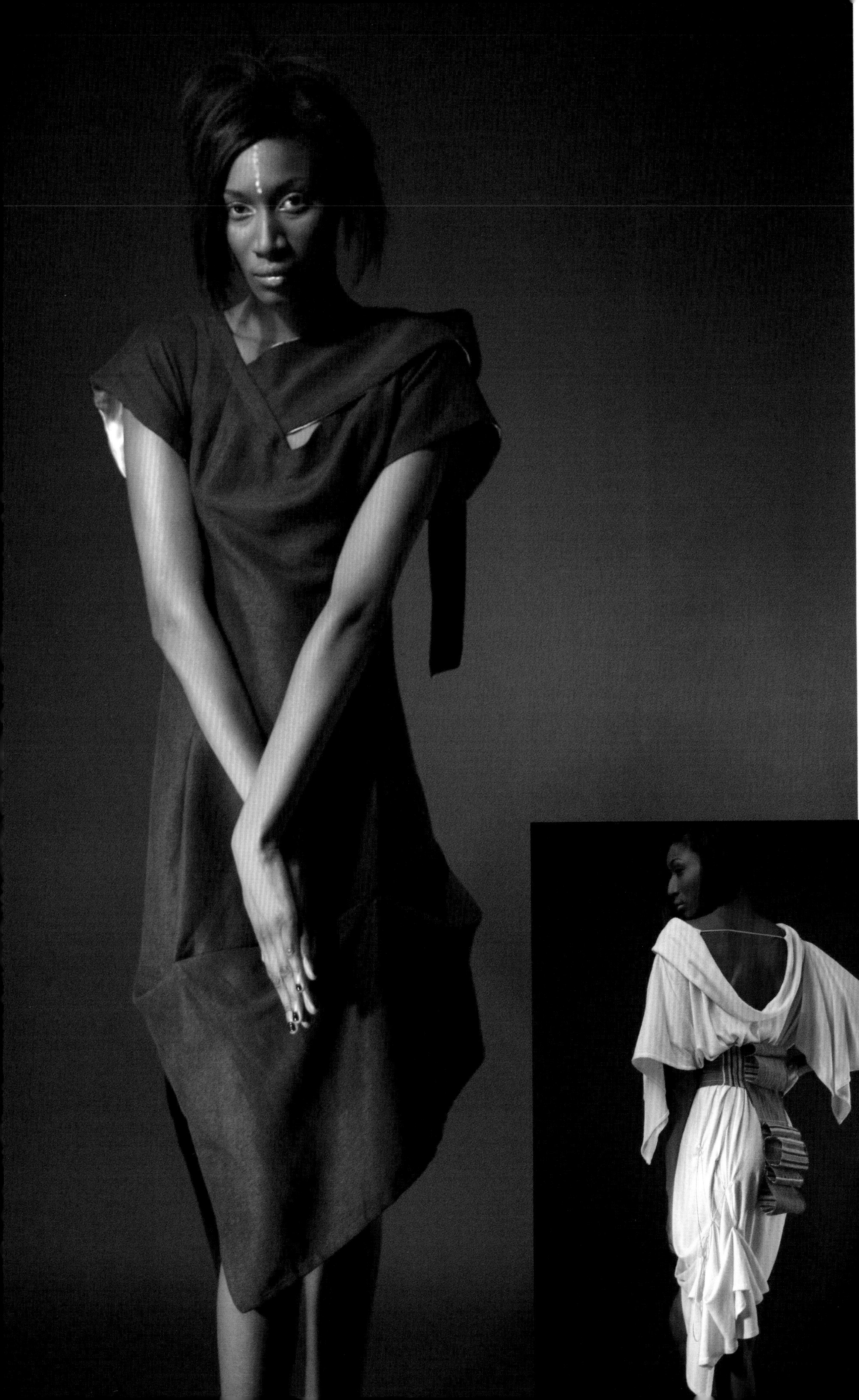

CHRISTINE BIRKLE

Owner of fashion label HUT UP founded in Berlin, Christine Birkle has caught the attention of such fashion luminaries as Dries Van Noten and Matteo Thun. She is a felter extraordinaire, renowned around the world for her creations, which are completely handcrafted using traditional felting and blocking methods. She practises a technique known as nuno felting ('nuno' is the Japanese word for 'cloth'), which uses a base fabric that is shaped and decorated by felting only selected areas. Beginning with minimally seamed garments in silk, linen or cotton, Birkle employs felting in place of darts, tucks and shaped seams to give the garments shape, form and dimension. Her clothing has an organic appearance in its shape and contours, and her soft refined pieces have richly detailed and understated textures. There are no consistent thicknesses, no straight corners and everything is organic. Birkle's designs have the sophistication of Miuccia Prada and the retro sensibility of Paul Poiret.

Nuno felting was made popular in the early 1990s by attempts to create sheer lightweight felt. The process of felt-making is tedious and requires an enormous amount of labour: pulling fibre, wetting it, soaping it up and 'walking' it until the fibres become matted and integrate themselves into the base fabric as well as one another, which can take hours. Despite the laborious nature of the work, felt needs very careful monitoring during the shrinking process to ensure an even texture and the right size and shape. Birkle manages through this labour-intensive craft to bring to life organic, crafted yet fashionable and unique pieces of clothing that capture a wonderful artisanal quality. She is the rare combination of an artist, a crafter and a successful fashion designer, and has gone on to pioneer this type of felting. As she explains, 'The ingredients are extra-fine merino wool, water and power.'

It was not until Birkle was a fashion and product design student in Berlin that she discovered felt. She elaborates on her love of the material: 'Felt is very flexible. You can produce any form with it. It can keep you cool as well as warm, and it's substantial, soft and decorative. The old stereotype of a crude material no longer makes sense today.' Birkle's first job was in the theatre to create the costumes for Yevgeny Schwartz's play *The Dragon*. She went on to create fantastical sculptural hats and then expanded into clothing and fashion accessories. She has shown her collections in Paris, Milan and London. Not content with fashionable clothing, Birkle also produces childrenswear, pieces for the home and the office, stuffed animals and weddings. Her sketchbook is brimming with ideas. Opening her first store in Berlin, Birkle has a studio above the shop.

Birkle exhibits and sells around the world. Barneys and Henri Bendel in New York and Takashimaya in Japan stock her products, and they are also available in Paris and Milan as well as Berlin.

Renowned for her quirky clothing and accessories, Christine Birkle creates designs with a sense of humour, colour and style.

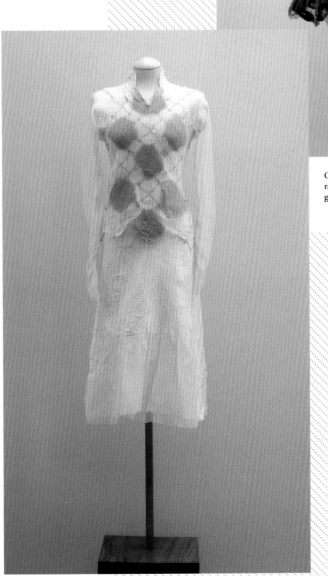

One of a kind, hand-felted pieces are fashioned from raw wool, silk, cotton and lace to create light, soft garments without seams or tucks by Christine Birkle.

CIEL

Sarah Ratty's ethical label Ciel is designed to make a more sustainable and environmental choice available to fashion-conscious women. Equally passionate about fashion as the environment, Ratty creates collections that reflect wit and style while incorporating a full range of luxury contemporary casual wear made from organic cotton, linen, wool and hemp. With a diverse selection of influences – Biba, art nouveau, 1940s style, the Bauhaus, Japanese kimono prints – Ciel is a blend of romantic, edgy and stylish shapes. Super-soft organic baby-alpaca knits in a wide range of natural colours are hand knitted in Peru. Silk hand-blocked prints made by Indian artisans and fair trade hand embroideries feature in the collections, as do bamboo, soy and silk dresses and separates. All items are produced using natural, sustainable and organic GOTS-and Eco-Tex-certified textiles, 100 per cent-azo-free dyes and recycled and recyclable fabrics. Ciel also offers a fun and playful lingerie and loungewear collection made from organic cotton seductively trimmed with French lace. All cotton for the lingerie is organically farmed in Turkey, and the whole process vertically integrated from the field to the end product. As Ratty explains: 'We make beautiful stylish clothes that don't sacrifice style for content, that give the satisfaction of knowing that you have made a difference whilst still looking and feeling great!'

Ratty describes Ciel as 'designing from the inside out', and has an integrated eco-design philosophy that pays attention to the small details, like garment labels and tags, as well as to the big picture, such as end life and end user considerations. The collection is environmentally and ethically produced, with all stages of manufacture tested and approved by respected third-party certification bodies, ensuring fair labour laws and ecological standards are complied with. Ciel has a policy of using local products to reduce transport emissions and operates a carbon-neutral offsetting programme. Sarah Ratty is also an advisor to the Soil Association Textile Advisory Committee and works as an eco-design consultant. Her goal is to 'create a 100 per cent ethical product base'.

Ciel is stocked in designer boutiques and stores across the UK, as well as in the USA and Japan. It is also sold through its own website. The fashion label attracts an A-list celebrity following, with Sienna Miller, Peaches Geldof and Cate Blanchett among its fans. Ciel was shortlisted for the 2007 *Observer* newspaper's Ethical Award and has been featured in *Elle* magazine, *Marie Claire* and *Vogue*.

Organic baby alpaca forms super-soft knits, hand knitted in Peru along with organic cotton and linen, fashioned into romantic, edgy designs by Ciel.

EMILY KATZ

Emily Katz owns and operates her own organic and sustainable clothing line, first under the label Bonnie Heart Clyde and now under her own name. As her design life flourishes, with multiple regional trade shows and events, Katz has found new opportunities for her first love – music – to coexist with her design life. In what is an increasing trend, young artists rarely satisfy themselves with a single expression of their creativity. In a similar vein, designer, artist, musician and activist, Katz designs stylish sustainable clothing and jewellery and fronts the Portland, Oregon, band Love Menu, also made up of artist, designers and musicians. Love Menu, a group built around Katz's lyrical songwriting and rich voice, produces delicate nouveau-folk compositions. Katz is confident that her two artistic endeavours can coexist, even on band tours: 'The thing that's been really great about doing the music and traveling with it, is that I can do my clothing sales at the same time.'

Born in the dessert hills of Tucson, Arizona, Katz was named after Simon & Garfunkel's 'For Emily, Whenever I May Find Her'. Growing up playing in rivers and libraries to fuel her creativity, Katz represents a creative anomaly – a self-supporting artist in a city where most artists support their creativity with a service job.

After studying at the Maryland Institute College of Art in Baltimore and returning to Portland, Katz's first clothing line, Bonnie Heart Clyde, was a crafty and whimsical collection of separates for men and women. The collection in her own name shows how the designer has grown up. Emily Katz clothes are sophisticated and understated, sustainable, elegant and practical. They feature intricate wraps and drapes in comfortable organic jersey or body-skimming liquid-metallic Lycra®, as well as silk crêpe de Chine, soya and wool. Deceptively simple dresses in monochromatic colours mask complex cutting and draping techniques. Tone-on-tone separates have a sporty edge and combine comfort with an urban sensibility. The 26-year-old designer juxtaposes diaphanous dresses with hard-wearing urban pieces, striving to create a niche in the fashion industry as well as become a design staple in your closet!

Available in boutiques across the USA and Canada, the Emily Katz collection is also sold online. She participates in many group shows and has been featured in such magazines as *Lucky*, *Nylon*, *Daily Candy* and *The Cutting Edge*.

Designer, artist, musician and activist, Katz creates organic fluid jersey dresses and hip, hard-wearing urban separates.

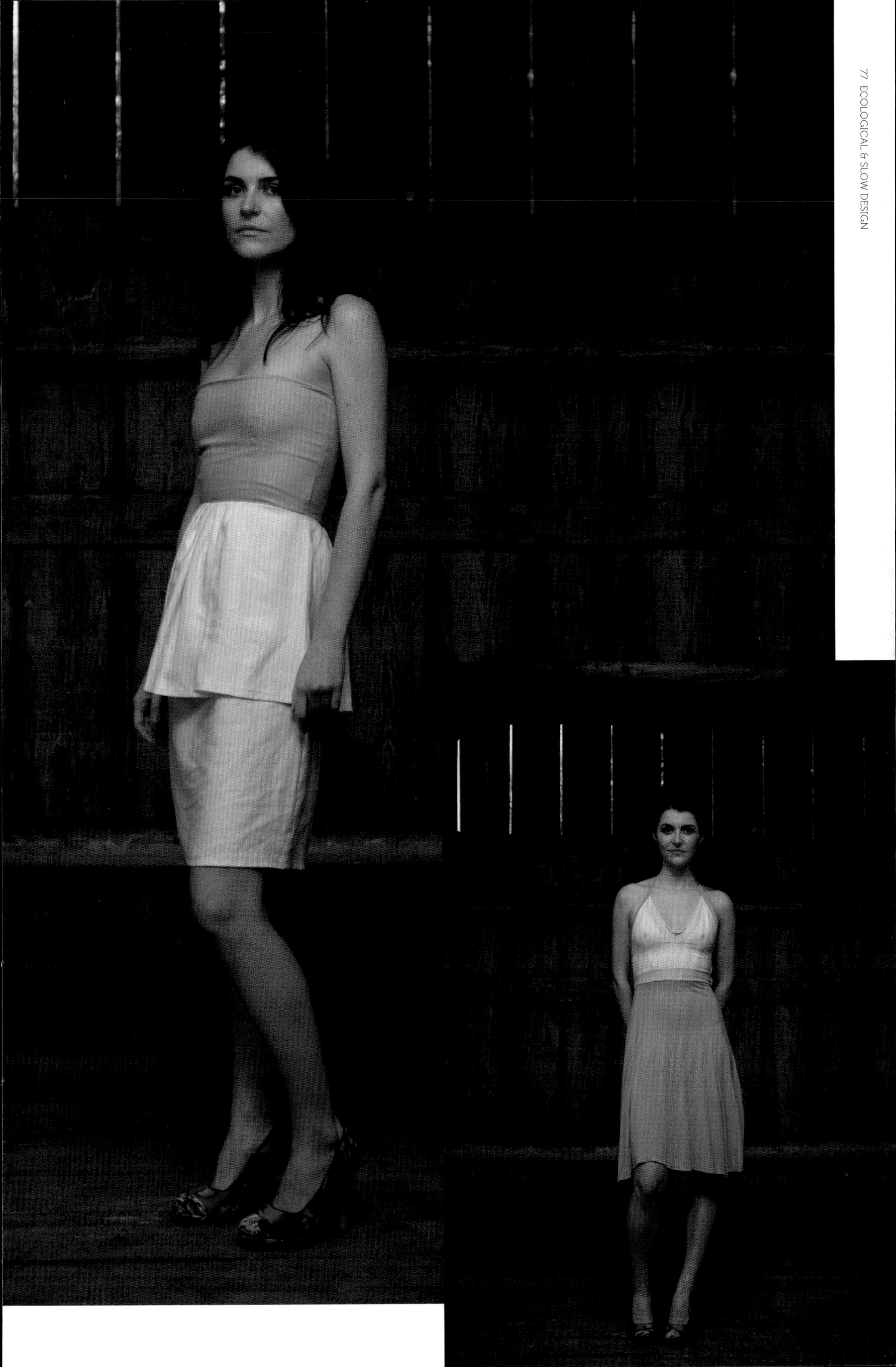

ENAMORE

A creative fashion label, Enamore produces clothing, lingerie and accessories made from the finest organic and sustainable fabrics, all sourced from accredited suppliers: 'Our collections are produced in the UK from the finest organic hemp, soya, cotton, silk and hand-selected vintage fabrics.' The collection is designed and produced in Bath, Wales and London, where employees are paid a fair wage and have regular working hours. Local outworkers are also employed to fulfil small orders. The label came into being in the seaside city of Brighton in 2004 thanks to founder Jenny Ambrose's love of vintage patterns and prints.

After discovering the damaging effects of the fashion industry on the environment, Ambrose's vision was to create beautiful, playful and quirky garments from organic fabrics and vintage materials. The label began as a small range of clothing made from hemp and colourful sourced prints from the 1950s and 1960s. It has since evolved into a diverse collection of dresses, separates and organic lingerie. There are influences of a modern-day version of the Vargas pin-up girl and naughty French maids' outfits in the lingerie, which is trimmed with vintage lace.

The collections are not based on a seasonal theme, with new designs replacing old each season; instead, popular styles form the basis of the line, while less popular pieces are sold off and replaced with new ones. All the fabrics used are at least 55 per cent organic or they are recycled vintage fabrics, while all dyes are azo-free. Hemp and hemp-blend fabrics are sourced in China, silk and organic cotton from India. The organic cotton is certified by SKAL; hemp cannot be certified, although it naturally requires little water and does not use pesticides or herbicides in its production cycle. Each new collection contains a greater proportion of certified organic materials than the previous one, and Ambrose strives to use the most sustainable fabrics each year. While the label is hoping to achieve certification of its ethical and sustainable credentials, it is difficult due to the broad variety of fabrics used. Interested in exploring new textiles like bamboo, Ambrose is always open to new products, fabrics and innovations. Textile waste, paper, card, metals and plastics are all recycled, and unused and unwanted fabrics and other materials are donated to local schools and colleges for art and educational purposes.

Enamore has featured in many TV broadcasts across various networks and the label's products retail across the UK, Europe and the USA and are available online.

Enamore's playful, quirky, retro-inspired clothing, lingerie and accessories are made from the finest sustainable and organic fabrics and hand-selected vintage finds.

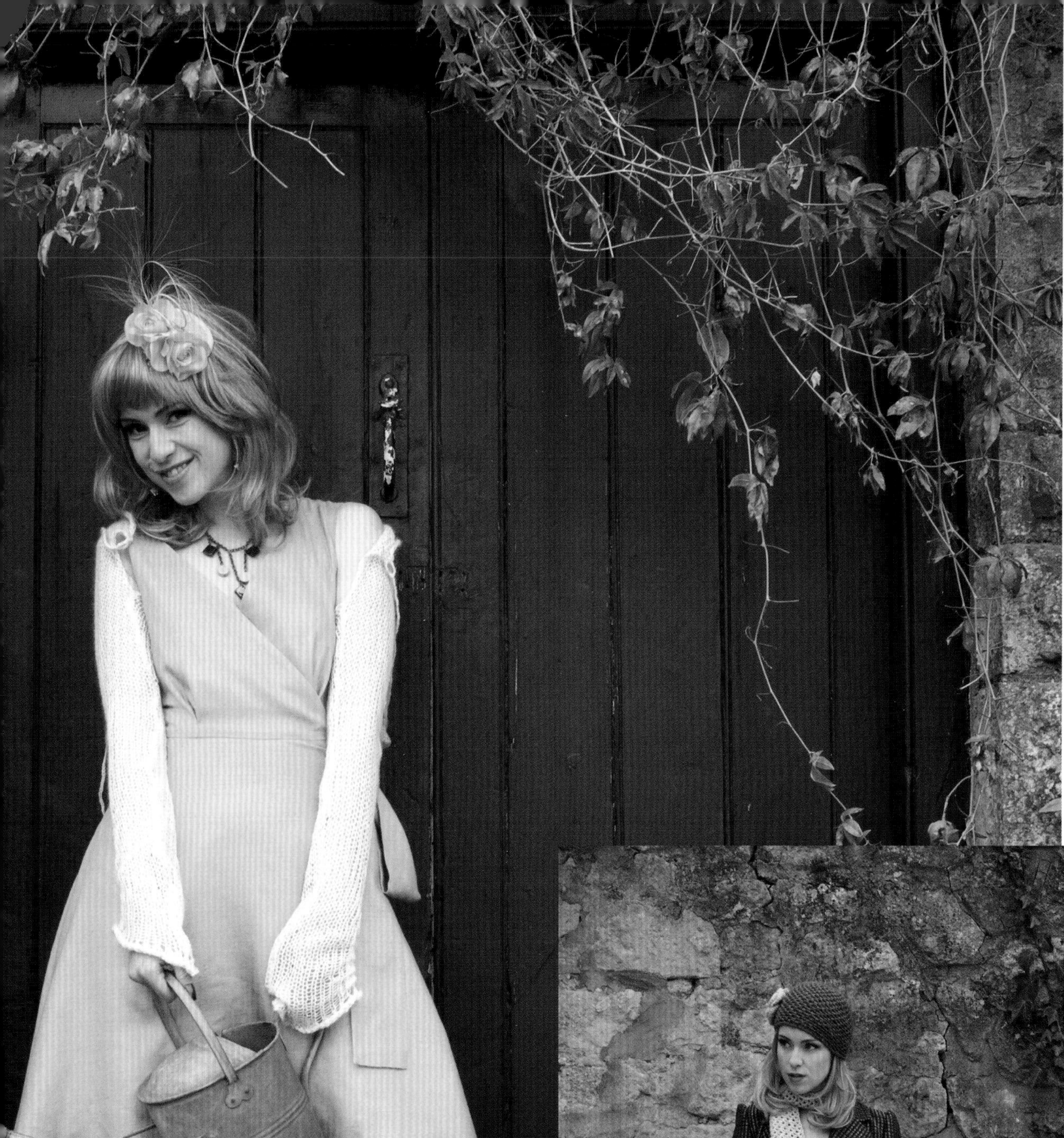

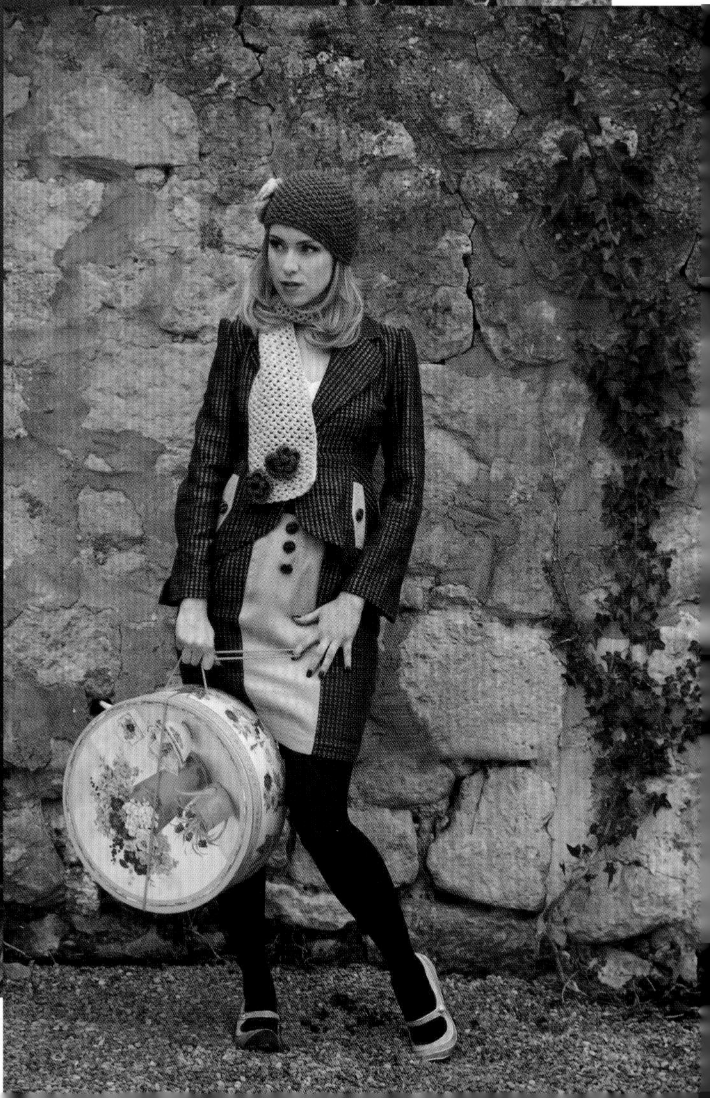

FIN

Based in Oslo, Norway, and striking a balance between edgy and classic, FIN presents graphic knitwear in casually wearable styles that punctuates a classic collection of sportswear, with fine jersey tops, pleated dress shorts and luxurious jersey wrap dresses. Head designer Per Age Sivertsen gives a nod to the past with his elegant sportswear collection. Employing organic fabrics, including wild hand-spun silk for texture, bamboo jersey for drape, organic Pima cotton for crisp sophistication and organic baby alpaca for rarity and luxury, FIN explores new designs and environmentally and socially responsible ideas in fashion production.

The label states: 'On our path, towards unique results, every step is of equal importance. We carefully select our materials to achieve the finest expression.' To recognize the hard labour that has gone into the production of the fabric as well as the clothes, FIN uses only fair trade-certified cotton, which contributes to a healthy environment and better working conditions for cotton producers. The spinning, dyeing and finishing of FIN's yarns is also carried out according to ecological standards. Organic-certified baby alpaca, one of the rarest and most luxurious fibres available, is incredibly soft, warm and silky to the touch and is incorporated into the collection in the form of sumptuous knits. The alpaca graze and roam freely on pesticide-free land, and the fleece from the baby alpaca is the most exclusive and beautiful. Wild silk is grown naturally and is hand-picked and hand-spun by artisans to create rich textural fabrics. While conventional silk production requires the larva to be killed at the pupa stage, the production of non-violent silk allows the pupa to mature into a free silk moth.

'When the idea of FIN was conceived, we set out on a path that has led us to so many different corners of the world and now involves a lot of people.' The company requires that all who work with them are concerned about wages, working hours, human rights and social accountability, and all their suppliers comply with their code of conduct. The brand believes in taking responsibility for its actions, so FIN invests in climate credits based on the carbon dioxide emissions calculated on the production and shipping of their garments, and with the aim of reaching carbon neutrality. The funds are then reinvested into renewable energy production in the countries where they produce. They explain: 'The social conditions behind our brand have been our focus since FIN's inception.'

Introducing an accessories line in autumn 2008, FIN now also produce a range of hand-embroidered wild silk shawls and alpaca scarves to complement the ready-to-wear collection. Showing and selling the brand in Berlin, Amsterdam, Copenhagen, Oslo, Paris and New York, FIN has garnered the support of fashion fans Keira Knightley and Kate Bosworth.

Sensuous, tactile, with a hint of boho chic, FIN uses innovative environmental fabrications and socially sustainable production methodology, combined with voluminous silhouettes and intricate pleats for the basis of the collection.

FRANÇOISE HOFFMANN

French felt-maker Françoise Hoffmann works in a three-dimensional collage of felt and fabric known as nuno felting, a technique of embedding fabrics to make felt. Based in Lyon, Hoffmann designs using many of the local textiles for which the city is famous, including silk chiffon, velvet, linen, cotton lace and other sumptuous fabrics. Hoffmann interprets the traditional process, using highly innovative combinations of fabric, print and graphic imagery. She digitally prints her fabrics, often sheer silk chiffon, with slightly enlarged text and images to compensate for the shrinkage that occurs during the felting process. The use of digital graphic imagery is something quite unique to Hoffmann's work. Playing with texture, colour, print and digital imagery, she works with her materials much like an artist with paint and spatula on a canvas. Her creations come into being through the labour-intensive ancient manual technique of milling wool and assimilating fibre. Nuno felting allows Hoffmann to work with textiles yet eliminate seams and darts, making it possible to make three-dimensional pieces without sewing.

Hoffmann begins with a two-dimensional pattern cut from thick plastic sheeting, which separates the front from the back of the garments as the two are felted as one at the same time, with only the plastic keeping them apart. One of the many unique features of felt is that the fabric is created at the same time as the design. Putting down a composition of silk fabrics, Hoffmann overlays and connects them with tufts of coloured merino wool, then wets the materials and begins to felt. Anticipating the interactions of each of the components – the wool shrinks, but the silk does not – Hoffmann must envisage the final effect, as well as work from the back side of the fabric and predict the migration of the fibres from the side they start on to the side they end up on. She must also be careful to maintain the soft hand of the silks and not overwork the felt, while at the same time ensuring that all the fibres are firmly embedded – a fine balance to achieve.

After studying at the Institut d'Etudes Théâtrales, part of the Sorbonne University, Hoffmann worked for ten years as an actress and director. Deciding in the mid-1990s to refocus her career on a more manual activity, she studied millinery at the atelier and hat museum in Chazelles-sur-Lyon and at the studio of Philippe Model, where she first discovered felting. Now, with her own felting studio in the Lyon hills, Hoffmann works on artists' projects as well as on one-off pieces for a wide range of customers, including Lanvin, for whom she created a velvet jacquard. She also made theatre costumes for Richard Wagner's *Lohengrin* at the Opéra de Lyon. Hoffmann's creations have been purchased by La Piscine, a museum dedicated to art and industry in Roubaix and The Cooper-Hewitt, National Design Museum in New York.

Combining wool felt, silk, velvet, linen, lace, cotton and graphic imagery, Hoffmann creates nuno-felted one-of-a-kind pieces.

LINDA LOUDERMILK

A flair for the dramatic comes naturally to Linda Loudermilk, who studied Shakespeare and costume design at Oxford University in the UK. Her intuitive sense of tailoring was inherited from her couturier grandmother. After practising as a sculptor, Loudermilk honed her design skills at The Art Institute of Colorado where she studied fashion, and on the Paris runway, before returning to Los Angeles to launch Linda Loudermilk and with it the luxury eco-movement.

The full name of Loudermilk's line, 'Linda Loudermilk Luxury Eco', is a reference to the label's designer roots and the groundbreaking work Loudermilk has done in establishing luxury eco in a world that only recognized hemp drawstring pants as ecological clothing. As one of the premier eco-lines, the company has been working with sustainable fabrics in high-end design for a lot longer than the current trend of ecological fashion. Her label seeks to redefine sustainability and design by giving back to the earth; it is 'an infusion of hope for an abused but resilient planet. Luxury eco is an emergency survival plan, fueled by design.'

Nature is the creative source for all of Loudermilk's designs. She channels nature's energy into graceful, unpredictable clothes. But, nature is not Loudermilk's quiet muse, rather it is a tormenting, awe-inspiring and ever-present reference and inspiration in her work. She explains: 'All that vastness, all those numberless small symmetries, all the brutality and fragility. Nature may be beautiful, but nature is not pretty. Nature is the original punk.'

When Loudermilk patterns a jacket after a waterfall, it's not about making something pretty to wear; it's about 'holy fearsome awe'. Likewise, the luxury eco category that Loudermilk invented with the launch of her line was not inspired by a sense of patchouli-smelling do-goodery. The sustainable fabrics she develops and sources reflect →

Linda Loudermilk creates luxury eco clothing, intricately interweaving sustainable fabrics woven from natural sources, such as bamboo and SeaCell® with her hallmark rock and roll, earth warrior style.

'All that vastness, all those numberless small symmetries, all the brutality and fragility. Nature may be beautiful, but nature is not pretty. Nature is the original punk.'

Loudermilk's dramatic, yet intricate, sense of design and flair incorporates rich textural details and graphic prints combined in sheer and solid combinations.

the respect she has for nature. Her clothes honour the ethos of nature, and then go back into the earth. Fabrics are made of sasawashi, bamboo, SeaCell®, soya and other exotic self-sustaining plants. Loudermilk believes that there is no need to sacrifice style, because if nature does not make apologies, then neither should the people who fortify, fear and believe in it. As for style, forget hemp tunics. In fact, forget hemp entirely. Loudermilk's line is all about refinement: polished, put-together looks that happen to be made from sustainable fabrics. These are clothes that pack an iconoclastic punch. She elaborates: 'The clothing and accessories we wear, the products we use and the vehicles we drive are a perfect conduit for the spirit of this complex, colorful and rockin' earth: this is luxury eco.'

Linda Loudermilk clothing outfits the fashion-conscious earth warriors within the eco-movement. The company offers eco-glamour, a fabulous look and an attitude that stops traffic and shouts the message: 'eco can be edgy, loud, fun, playful, feminine (or not) and hyper-cool.' The collection is meticulously created and researched using sustainable business practices and fair-labour standards. Sustainable style is terra incognita, but for Loudermilk, the pioneering has only just begun. Like nature itself, she has more foundations to shake: 'We are one. Join the journey. Shake your foundation.'

The line is sold through an extensive range of boutiques across the USA, as well as in Canada and Denmark. It is also available through online retailers.

MAGDALENA SCHAFFRIN

Magdalena Schaffrin produces an eco-luxury collection of women's and men's separates. In a world where modern luxury is about time, quality and conscience, she offers a collection that encompasses all three by investing time in her product and in the process of design and manufacture and by letting her conscience dictate her choices. Schaffrin only uses natural fibres, mostly with organic and environmental certification, sourced from Germany, Switzerland, France and Austria. All production is carried out in Berlin, and she guarantees fair working conditions and minimizes her carbon footprint. For Schaffrin, eco-luxury is the result of quality awareness, a sustainable design concept and the use of renewable and ecological materials. She explains: 'Today, our way of living and consuming is mostly characterized by the loss of time and cheap prices. The damage done to the environment and people is huge.'

On finishing her fashion schooling at the Berlin University of the Arts, Schaffrin founded her own-name label in 2007, motivated by her inability to find a design position with a socially responsible fashion label. Designs feature classic timeless styles, strict lines and clear shapes. Schaffrin shows her collection once a year, instead of the usual two or four times, concentrating on the development and production of a single line, where items can be ordered in summer or winter weights. This results in a range of classic items intended to last and not go out of fashion. Core items are repeated season after season to emphasize the longevity of the styling, as well as to minimize waste and overproduction. Her already small carbon footprint is further reduced through minimal packaging and the shipping of garments in recycled paper and recycled boxes. Schaffrin describes her thinking: 'If fine and eco-friendly fabrics merge into high-quality clothing, which get worn for a long time, the clothing becomes durable. If a piece of clothing is durable and the resources are grown according to ecological guidelines, it becomes sustainable.'

Schaffrin also founded the GREENshowroom with partner Jana Keller (see page 92) to present a range of green luxury labels and lifestyle products during fashion week. Their own experiences at trade and fashion shows – where they were either placed between yoga clothing and cotton bags at eco-fairs, or sandwiched between 'unethical' labels at 'regular' fashion fairs – led them to understand the necessity for an up-market venue that understood their ethics but also placed them with other high-end brands. Hence, the formation of the GREENshowroom.

Schaffrin now presents her collections in Berlin, Paris and Copenhagen, and was chosen to take part in the sustainable fashion-design project 'Next Vision: Bright Green Fashion'. Her collection 'Twins' won a competition run by Galeries Lafayette, which also sells her line. Schaffrin's clothing is available in high-end boutiques across Germany and also through her own website.

Moderately extravagant, timeless, classic pieces are produced by Schaffrin using organic materials and designed to be worn for a long time.

Magdalena Schaffrin produces a single collection a year, with each style available in both light- and heavy-weight fabrications.

ROYALBLUSH

RoyalBLUSH produces a collection of handbags and jewellery for the ecologically responsible. Designed by Jana Keller and inspired by the Swiss Alps, the multifunctional handbags are as practical as they are unique. Keller explains: 'The importance lies in the design and functionality, while sustainable work ethics are natural.' The soft, pliable bags come in all shapes and sizes and incorporate her signature braiding and interwoven details entirely created by hand. Each bag is made from vegetable-tanned leather, which is tanned with tree bark in place of the usual chemicals. Vegetable tanning is an artisan tradition handed down the generations for over 200 years, and now uses both antique recipes and state-of-the-art technology. The transformation from raw hides happens slowly in wooden drums, an astonishing process based on the use of natural tannins extracted from chestnut or Argentinean quebracho trees, on modern technologies and machineries and on the slow passing of time. Nearly 40 days are needed to transform raw hides into unique vegetable-tanned leathers, which absorb the traces of our life, aging with a unique character.

Using only the best calf leather from Italy, the vegetable-tanned leather is treated with herbs and roots and continues to age naturally with wear, sun and rain exposure. In turn, this creates a natural protection for the bag, an individual patina, a pleasant scent and varies the colour as well as the texture from one piece to the next. The interiors of the bags are made out of recycled and pressed leather leftovers. RoyalBLUSH only works with suppliers based in the European Union and Switzerland, choosing to support the local economy and keep carbon dioxide emissions low.

Originally trained as a fashion designer, Keller acquired a taste for designing accessories in vegetable-dyed leather when working on her own womenswear graduate collection. Showcasing the collection in Germany, Paris and Italy, she hand sewed each bag on her domestic 1950s sewing machine. With few accessories and, in particular, handbag manufacturers offering sustainable products, Keller recognized a gap in the market and decided to focus on an accessories line. She has expanded her brand to include a jewellery line to match the bags. High-fashion handbags, the 'it' item of the fashion arena, have excluded eco-design thus far with the very occasional exception.

Constantly striving to make the bags as natural as possible – 'You could put our bag in the compost, and all that's left are the metal buckles' – one of the offshoots of the all-natural production is an extremely lightweight bag. Organic cotton and peace silk are used as lining for the bags, cautchuck for padding, cotton wick for handles and old brushed brass for the metal closures. Each item is made to order, eliminating waste and overproduction.

Keller founded the GREENshowroom with partner Magdalena Schaffrin (see page 88). They offer a platform for other like-minded eco-conscious high-end lifestyle brands to showcase their products during fashion week in Berlin. RoyalBLUSH sells across Europe, Japan and the USA, as well as online through their independent website.

Vegetable-tanned calf leather with its unique patina, scent and character are worked into a line of alpine inspired bags by RoyalBLUSH.

SAMANT CHAUHAN

An alumnus of the National Institute of Fashion and Technology (NIFT), New Delhi, Samant Chauhan made an impact at international level when he was selected by his Alma Mater to represent them at Singapore Fashion Week. As a consequence of winning the first runner-up in the Asian Young Designer Contest, he was awarded US$5,000 (£3,000), which he used to realize his dream of starting his own label. Coming from a small town in the state of Bihar and a completely non-fashion background, he had always aspired to the world of glamour and fashion. The son of an Indian railway employee, he attended NIFT's knitwear design programme for fashion studies, while undertaking projects for local and exporting fashion houses to make ends meet.

Working predominately with natural fibres, and silk in particular, Chauhan specializes in unusual silk yarns with minimal embellishment. Taking up the challenge to revitalize the languishing hand-loom industry in his home town of Bhagalpur, Chauhan presents a contemporary take on traditional Bhagalpur silk, showcasing its unique beauty to a global audience through its exclusive use in his collections. Textural, asymmetric and with an earthy organic quality, the pieces possess a sensuality that evokes wood nymphs and Shakespeare's *A Midsummer Night's Dream*.

Explaining his relationship with silk, Chauhan says: 'Silk is a metaphor for me, an indirect way of going back to my roots and bringing to the present the essence of my past, and transplanting it into Bhagalpur soil.' From the hand-loomed weave designs to the final items, Chauhan designs everything with an international audience in mind. The line, consisting of handwoven and knitted 100 per cent raw silk, linen and cotton-linen blends, uses only eco-friendly dyes and processes. Inspired by Asian fashions, Chauhan bridges the gap between East and West, fusing the two paradigms to create one unique look. Exploring such themes as the *Karma Sutra*, he delves into the eroticism prevalent in ancient Indian art. Layers of fabric entangle to symbolize a lovers' embrace, while fabric drapes and clings to the body. Colours are taken from an earthy palette, with textures created through the use of unusual silk yarns and weaves. Chauhan elaborates: 'My quest to unravel the mystique of the most celebrated erotica ever written, Vatsayana's *Karma Sutra*, written in 4BC. It formed the inspiration for the erotic sculptures of the later ancient temples of India.'

Samant Chauhan's work has evolved over the years, and his appreciation of silk grows. He sells through several high-profile designer stores in the USA, Israel, Moscow, London and Singapore, and presents his collections at both Delhi and London fashion weeks.

Using 100 per cent raw silk, linen and cotton-linen blends, hand-loomed in Bhagalpur, India, Samant Chauhan is known for his textured fabrics created from the use of unusual silk yarns.

U ROADS

Creating shoes made from post-consumer recycled materials, U Roads crafts soles and trimmings from used rubber tyres and from recycled leathers, papers and other materials that reduce environmental degradation. The shoes are entirely handcrafted, from the cutting and stitching to the washing processes, and each detail is designed by shoe stylist Bruno Bordese and manufactured according to the Italian handcraft tradition. The company is 'taking steps towards a better planet'.

U Roads is a moral project based around a group of people committed to their mission of creating something new without compromise while preserving the environment and helping to control pollution. U Roads explains: 'Recycling a product or material that has already had a life of its own gives a second life to the new object, and in so doing, also gives this new article a soul of its own. We can think of U Roads as shoes with souls.'

Working with the United Nations Environment Programme (UNEP), U Roads believes that people must take the lead in building sustainable development: 'We have learned that words of concern must be matched by action. We have only one Earth. We do not have a single moment to spare.' Everyday actions, from conserving electricity to planting trees and from buying 'green' products to recycling, are the backbone of the struggle to save our earth from the ecological crisis of ozone depletion, greenhouse gases, the extinction of plants and animals and overflowing landfill sites.

The brand's designs have a unique sense of style. Fashion is not the defining factor, but people sharing their way of thinking is their inspiration, and the production of a tough, durable and functional product is their intent: 'U Roads has a strong soul. Clean, unique, coherent. An ethical choice. A strong choice. A style choice.' Collections are seasonal and updated, with tradition at their core. The shoes and boots have lots of character, looking from new as if they are old well-loved favourites, the kind you turn to every day for comfort as well as style and imbued with meaning and character through daily wear. Using worn vintage and garment-washed leathers, the footwear has a raw retro feel to it. Each style pays homage to the past through its skilled, handmade and artisanal craftsmanship, while also having a unique urban sensibility. Every pair of shoes and boots carries the recycle symbol imprinted on the heel, proudly displaying its brand to the world.

Boutiques across Eastern and Western Europe, Japan, Australia and the USA stock the shoes and boots. U Road's Facebook page and blog reflect the cool, urban, hip aesthetic that the shoes and boots exude.

U Roads utilizes post-consumer recycled materials to produce a collection of shoes and boots with character.

YOJ

Yoj is a research collection, conceived and designed by Laura Strambi following her extensive research on natural textile production and organic dyes. With a philosophy that we must live and work responsibly, she is sensitive to renewable energy resources and the control of production of materials. Yoj only uses materials that have been produced with respect to nature and to mankind by using biological fibres and natural dyes. Each item is unique and completely handmade in every phase of production, from concept to finished garment.

The name 'Yoj' is a graphic synthesis of the brand's concept. Inspired by ancient Sanskrit texts, each letter of the name stands for a concept and idea. 'Y' is for 'yoga' and the Sanskrit root of the word, which means 'union'. 'O' represents the centre, a perfect circle, complete in its own right. 'J' is for 'jewel' and stands for beauty, a concept born of emotion. The collection is architectural in its form, using the shape and outline of the letters of the name 'Yoj' to inspire and restrict shape and form. Wide circles of fabric cut in wonderfully luxurious heavy cottons collapse on to and drape around the body in unexpected ways. The pieces form a whole that is futuristic in concept, yet retro in its aesthetic, while deceptively simple lines complement and cocoon the body.

Winter cotton, cotton and silk and cotton and bamboo blends, soya fibres and cashmere are all used in the garments. Biologically grown Pima cotton is certified and garments are manufactured in Italy. Colours are informed by the yoga concepts of calm and compatibility, combined with arduous research into vegetable dyeing and biological growth methodology. Complicated colour extractions and dyeing with herbal-tea infusions form the basis of the range, the results of which are wonderfully rich and complex variations of monochromatic hues, from natural white through grey to black.

Strambi is passionate about research into contemporary art, design and theatre, and has been instrumental in the organization of international trade fairs, such as Lineapelle in Milan, where she is on the fashion committee. She has also designed collections for Marina Rinaldi and Max Mara and costumes for opera performances. She is a visiting lecturer at the University of Bologna and contributed to the curriculum at Jedtepe University in Istanbul. The Yoj collections are available through high-end boutiques across Italy, the Far East and the USA.

With a focus on biological fibres and exhaustive research into textile dyeing, the Yoj collection is typified by the use of subdued and subtle coloration achieved through colour extraction and dyeing by decoction and herbal infusion.

Organic Pima cotton, soya, cashmere, silk jersey,
bamboo and natural wool are vegetable-dyed for the
sculptural, architectural lines of the Yoj collection.

Chapter Three

RECYCLE,
REUSE &
REDESIGN

The idea that second-hand and recycled items pass on their life experiences is what imbues redesigned clothing with its sense of value. When wearing a pre-owned item of clothing, it is as if you inherit a history of lived experiences. You benefit from each piece's own identity and character. The care and affection lavished on a well-loved piece of clothing remains with the item and is inherited and added to by new owners, giving each piece a life force of sorts that is almost tangible. This is the beauty and attraction of vintage, recycled and redesigned garments: the sense of history and of lives lived that they bring with them. The British, with their love of history and culture of craft, inevitably lead this area of eco-design, as it makes for the perfect combination of appreciation and skills. There are, nevertheless, some wonderful examples from other geographic locations that capitalize on their unique stories and customs.

Having grown out of, at least in part, our grandparents' 'make-do' culture of mending and repairing, redesign has moved well beyond its historic roots to make use of otherwise unwearable items of clothing by cutting, piecing and embellishing them to create entirely new pieces, in many cases more desirable than the originals. It is an idea that has found its time and its natural home in the street markets and boutiques of the UK. This practice has now expanded to include innovative items, designs and designers across the globe. In a fast-fashion universe of low-quality throwaway clothing, redesign is the ultimate expression of slow fashion, as each piece must be individually conceived and crafted from scratch. It has the added bonus of diverting items destined for landfill, the ultimate end for much of our discarded clothing. Companies such as TRAIDremade lead the way in this arena, with their retro sensibility and love of vintage. TRAID started as a charity shop before conceiving the idea of recutting and resewing quality pieces of clothing that otherwise would not sell due to stains and tears. Another example, Geoffrey B. Small exemplifies the unending design and creative possibilities of working with recycled garments and textiles. His work is at the forefront of cutting-edge avant-garde design in any arena, not just the recycled or reused world.

The average American throws away approximately 31 kilograms (68 pounds) of clothing and textiles per year, with about 85 per cent destined for landfills; in the UK, over 900,000 million items of clothing are discarded each year. Textiles present particular problems in landfill sites. Synthetic fibres do not decompose, while woollen garments do decompose but in so doing produce methane, which contributes to carbon dioxide emissions and global warming. Furthermore, the exportation of used clothing to the African continent has devastated their fledgling textile and clothing industries. A better argument could not be made for the value of recycling, reusing and redesigning than this.

Demano creates recycled courier bags from original bags featuring promotional banners.

ANGELA JOHNSON

An Arizona-based indie designer, Angela Johnson handcrafts quirky, playful, tongue-in-cheek clothes from recycled fabrics. With a sideshow meets vaudeville retro style, she draws inspiration from vintage circus costumes for her dresses, which have an element of coquettishness with equal measures of in-your-face showgirl and Victorian murder-mystery drama. Johnson produces a redesigned line of ballgowns, party and prom dresses made from recycled T-shirts. Sourcing her T-shirts from charity stores in the Arizona area, or from donations, she crafts unique one-off pieces. Customers often donate their entire T-shirt collections, which they have outgrown psychologically or physically, choosing to honour the part they played in their life story by having a custom-made T-shirt party dress created. T-shirt dresses form the basis of Johnson's line and styles are repeated year after year, although the T-shirts always change. She explains: 'The motivation to create my entire line out of recycled T-shirts came from the lack of fashion-industry resources in Arizona.'

Graphic prints adorn many of her designs with mixed and matched or juxtaposed mismatched fabric scraps. She produces an annual, rather than the more usual seasonal, collection of original, unique and limited-edition items. In addition to the recycled T-shirt line, Johnson also works extensively with men's button-down shirts, recycling them into myriad mismatched tops and bottoms. She also keeps a private customer base, for which she custom-makes individual pieces. Johnson says, 'Without wholesale fabric vendors and manufacturers at my disposal to use for mass production, I decided to create one-of-a-kind pieces from materials that are readily available and affordable in any state.'

After graduating from the Fashion Institute of Design and Merchandising (FIDM) in Los Angeles, Johnson started in the industry by designing for X-Large and X-Girl, both celebrity-owned clothing collections. Moving on to form her own collection, she founded a streetwear line called Monkeywench with celebrity Christie Clark from the US soap opera *Days of Our Lives*, and FIDM alumna Dana Wilson. Selling around the world and adorning celebrities like Pamela Anderson, Christina Applegate, Tori Spelling and Leann Rimes, the Monkeywench line has featured on various prime-time TV sitcoms and shows.

Moving back to Scottsdale, Arizona in 2004, Johnson founded her own collection under her name and began teaching at the New School for the Arts. With a loyal following of dedicated customers, she was honoured by the prestigious Fashion Group International as Arizona's Rising Star in 2004, and has a plethora of other recognitions and awards. Johnson has featured in many US-based newspapers and magazines, from *The Washington Post* to *Seventeen*, and on various TV shows and news reports. Johnson's designs can be found in a handful of actual and online boutiques, as well as through her website.

Indie designer Angela Johnson handcrafts
tongue-in-cheek prom dresses and ballgowns from
recycled T-shirts.

COSTUMISÉE PAR LIZA

Graciela Arico, an Argentinean from a Spanish-Italian family who has also lived in Brazil, Venezuela and now France, is the founder of Costumisée par Liza. Her Marais-based boutique in Paris specializes in vintage and new garments, jewellery, decorative items and accessories, each of which she has transformed in some exceptional way. Arico customizes each item herself, and the store is true to the spirit of the Marais district: individual, sometimes amusing and always sensual. Arico creates garments and objects that transcend their origin and capture a new spirit of design and originality. With a whimsical and artistic aesthetic, she has a sense of style that appeals to the individual not afraid to express herself through her clothing. Her daring sense of colour and wonderfully eclectic taste in pattern and print mean that her designs exude a love of life.

Arriving in France in 2002 with her French husband and two children, Arico created the brand Madame G, a line of customized vintage clothes and hand-painted, one-of-a-kind china and decorative objects that included accessories and costume jewellery. Costumisée par Liza is a logical extension of that experience, presented in a district famed for its eclecticism and acceptance of the avant-garde and the new.

Having lived in Argentina, Brazil and France, among other places, Arico is influenced by these and her experiences in them. She incorporates the powerful waves of Brazil, the scent of wet Argentinean pampas, the tango and the bustle of the Parisian metro into her highly individual work. In Argentina, her means of rebellion against political repression and her way of feeling free, alive and young was through the creation of clothing. She explains: 'I have done many things and lived in many countries, unconsciously…filtered into my personality; [are] sensations, colours, fragrances that belong [to] or reflect some of these places; each have knitted themselves into my soul and come out in my creations.'

Arico says, 'I started very young to change the look of my clothes, to show my true personality, to express myself.' This form of self-expression became her passion over the years, and she would customize garments by her favourite designers to better express her own vision of life. Motivated by childhood souvenirs and teenage memories, she conveys her understanding of femininity through her work. Arico works with found, discarded and unwanted objects and clothing, breathing new life into them and making them desirable again. She turns old ties into mobile-phone cases and mismatched buttons into bags.

Selling exclusively through her boutique in the Marais, Arico's work has also featured in *Marie Claire*.

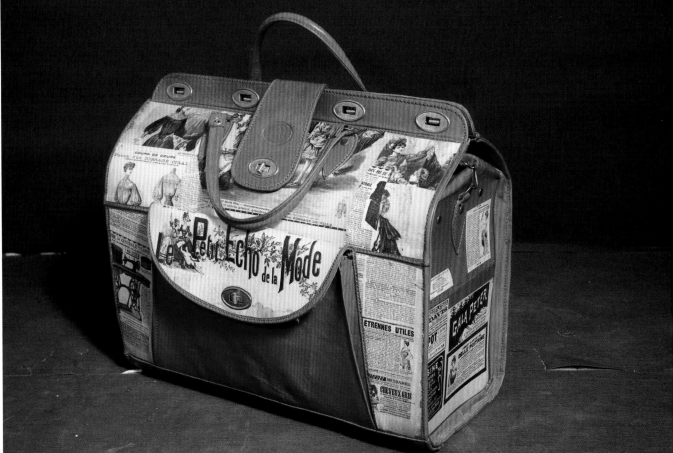

Customizing and transforming vintage and new garments, jewellery and accessories are transformed and customized in an individual, amusing and sensual way for the Costumisée par Liza collection.

DEMANO

Arriving in Barcelona from Bogotá, Colombia, Demano founders Liliana Andrade, Marcela Manrique and Eleonora Parachini were astonished by the number of promotional banners attached to the city's poles to promote exhibitions, events and cultural festivals. After a chance encounter with the workmen dismantling the banners, they realized the flexibility, strength and waterproof nature of the material and persuaded the workmen to let them have some of the discarded banners, out of which they made a few bags. Following rave reviews from their friends, they saw the potential of their idea and approached Barcelona City Hall with a proposal to recycle and reuse the banners by making them into courier bags. Demano then proceeded to make individual agreements with the producers, designers and artists for use of their images.

After obtaining and selecting the banners and getting creative clearance from the designers, they painstakingly clean each banner one by one, using orange rind as the cleaning agent. Working from digital photos, they experiment on the computer with various possible cut and shape combinations, before making samples. Due to their source material and the limited number of banners produced, their bags are limited editions, specific not just to a place – Barcelona – but also to the timing of an exhibition or cultural event. They explain: 'The main characteristic of Demano is that it works with materials that are harmless to the environment, producing unique objects, designer objects made for urban life, objects that tell a story and that were made in Barcelona.'

Although the project started with banners, Demano never intended them to be their only source material, as the concept was always to use city waste. They now also use the polyester construction nets that cover building façades, 1970s discarded clothing, cloth remnants and organic cotton to develop hats, shoes, stationery and T-shirts. Some projects are tailored to a specific client's needs, such as aprons for painting workshops at Barcelona's Museum of Contemporary Art.

With a background in architecture and art and no formal business training, Demano grew organically out of human capital, not financial investment, with the founding members supporting themselves through other employment. After establishing themselves formally in 2001, they were supported by Barcelona Activa with business-development mentoring, helping them to develop their first plan.

As the company has grown and their ideas developed, the designers have realized that they are defined by their values, not their products. The idea behind Demano is unique to Barcelona, with its rich cultural backdrop and character combined with the huge amount of waste it generates. They describe their brand as made from 'unique objects with a history, made in Barcelona and with an environmental awareness'.

Demano products were first stocked in museum shops because of the connection between the museums and their use of banners. They have since expanded into online sales as well as other retail outlets, with clothing and accessories retailers now constituting their major market. They sell in France, Italy, Portugal, Germany, the Netherlands, Denmark, the Czech Republic, Japan, Hong Kong, Singapore and Korea.

Demano create courier bags from discarded PVC
and polyester advertising materials from exhibitions,
festivals and cultural events.

E2

Michele Meunier and Olivier Chatenet are the founders of E2, a French label that specializes in refashioning vintage designer finds into contemporary, desirable and wearable pieces. With a celebrity following, including Madonna and Gwyneth Paltrow, and a by-appointment-only studio in Paris, they are exploring new directions with their label, outside the traditional fashion system, far removed from marketing and closer to the customer. Mixing contemporary styling with antique and ethnic heritage pieces, E2 offers individuality through its work. In tune with customers' dissatisfaction with the fashion system's delivery of spring styles in January and autumn collections in June, E2's styles are sold directly from the runway or showroom in season, making for a freshness impossible to obtain with the usual long lead times. Chatenet explains, 'Michele and I wanted to come up with an original way of thinking about fashion for independent, well-informed people.'

The collection is divided into groups and each piece is unique and customized. Reworked vintage items from the couture greats – Yves Saint Laurent Rive Gauche, Lanvin and Madame Grès – are either subtly altered or entirely re-created. Ethnic and folkloric costume is also reworked for a contemporary feel and created from scratch by the design duo. A unique collection of dresses made exclusively from vintage silk scarves rounds out the different groups. These are not simply handkerchief-point sundresses, but complex, subtle creations with a delicate interplay of colour and print. They believe, 'Just as new can become old, vintage can become new.'

They both have a history of working in couture for some of the stars of the industry through the 1980s and 1990s: Chanel, Thierry Mugler, Azzedine Alaïa and Comme des Garçons to name just a few. They first went into partnership in 1987; renowned for their minimalist design, Meunier and Chatenet were the masterminds behind the brand Maiot-Chanet. E2 was formed in 1999 as a means of exploring new directions in design that embraced their passion for classic vintage clothing. Sourcing items to rework from estate sales, auctions and flea markets, the pair prefer to showcase their work in an exhibition format rather than a fashion show, to best present the detailed workmanship and to allow customers to see their work up close and personal instead of breezing by them on a catwalk. Often creating unique one-of-a-kind items on a commission basis, they also produce items for exhibition and sale. In its first ten years, the atelier has grown from the original 2 to 25.

Garnering major press coverage in such magazines as *W*, *Luxx* and *Amica*, E2 can be bought online through the couture lab website, direct from their gallery-like shows or by appointment at their atelier in Paris.

E2 restore, rehabilitate and restyle vintage flea-market finds to their customers' preferences.

FRAU WAGNER

Frau Wagner turns vintage and unwanted clothing into one-of-a-kind desirable items. The worn garments are innovatively reconstructed into something completely new, using only the highest quality materials, such as silk, chiffon, organza, velvet and fur. The collection has a contemporary feel with sporty overtones that are reworked into sophisticated high-fashion items; for example, Nike stripes and ribbed active-wear cuffs become the finishing details on floaty silk dresses or feature in elegant halter-neck tops with crisp white collars and cuffs. Old discarded commodities become sought-after items: men's ties are reborn as swishing skirts, an old police uniform is reinterpreted as a lascivious bustier dress. A sense of humour and intellect permeates the collection with the juxtaposition of old and new, sporty and dressy, Grace Kelly and Amy Winehouse.

The Spring/Summer 09 collection focused on the reuse of sportswear items. Frau Wagner was attracted to the democratic nature of active sportswear, worn by street kids and athletes alike, with each item charged with feelings of joy, excitement and sweat. It thrilled Frau Wagner to make a couture evening dress from these items that were imbued with their past life of exercise and exertion, the social code understood around the world, thereby forming opposition to the elitist nature of high-end fashion through each and every piece in the collection. She explains: 'I process clothing with a distinctive social code, for example, uniforms, sportswear or gentlemen's shirts and look for an antithetic context.'

Upon completion, each item is named after its buyer, the concept being to personally brand each redesigned piece with an individual signature, and to simultaneously make an antithetical statement about global branding, when the exact same item is available in multiple locations with the brand DNA interwoven into every single design. With names like Frau Braun, Frau Mösch and Mrs Vita, the items are named as they are reworked, with the wearer, not the designer, deciding on the name, making an anachronistic statement through the renaming of old items reworked and re-presented as new pieces.

Documenting the entire process, Frau Wagner takes photographs that form the basis of her artwork. She creates digitized and solarized imagery by overlaying photographs of the buyers in their garments with print, pattern and colour to produce one-of-a-kind art around the one-of-a-kind garments. She makes fantastical fairy-tale statements about the wearer and their new purchase through the camera lens and through the reworking of the photographs, much in the same way as the clothes themselves are deconstructed and then reconstructed. Frau Wagner says, 'I love to tailor a blouse for Madonna that is made of Helge Schneider's underpants, or vice versa!'

Frau Wagner sells through her own atelier in Kreuzberg, Berlin, and her work has featured on German television, in print in *Zitty*, *Tip* and *Vital* magazines and on the Goethe Institute website.

Active sportswear, uniforms and men's shirts are
combined with chiffon and organza to create radically
redesigned dresses by Frau Wagner.

FROM SOMEWHERE

Born of an abiding love of vintage, provincial haberdasheries, beautiful clothes and exquisite artisanship, From Somewhere began trading in 1997 with a small capsule collection of second-hand sweaters and cardigans rescued from landfill and individually customized with elaborate crochet detailing. Originally sold exclusively at The Cross boutique in London's Notting Hill, the designs were noticed within months by buyers, nationally and internationally, and started selling all over the world.

From Somewhere patiently reclaims fabrics collected from cutting-room floors and the fashion industry's dustbins. Designed by Orsola de Castro and Filippo Ricci, the collections are made with luxury designer pre-consumer waste, such as swatches, strike offs, sample yardage and production ends. Upcycling high-end fashion textile waste into beautiful clothes, From Somewhere rethinks the fashion industry's waste, rescuing textiles as a design solution to an environmental problem. Recovering fabrics from Italy's manufacturers, they particularly love to work with cashmere, menswear fabrics and high-tech sportswear textiles. The designers explain: 'We used to have to really convince the manufacturers to give us their leftovers, but now we are approached by companies wanting to achieve a creative waste management as part of their "greenification".'

Each piece is individually cut and incorporates an original use of colour and panelling, making From Somewhere pieces instantly recognizable. The beauty of each piece lies in its uncompromising balance between contemporary design and a poetic and ethical solution to pre-consumer waste. Inspired by ballrooms, English gentlemen and naughty secretaries, From Somewhere's collections embody →

From Somewhere's unique pieces are the result of upcycling high-end fashion and textile surplus, such as swatches, production off-cuts and end of rolls.

ladylike sophistication with a playful edge. Fitted and floaty dresses, tailored coats, skirts and trousers, quirky little jumpers and tops are made with a devotion to detail and visual eclecticism. Taking full advantage of the unusual origins of the textiles, the designers 'redream' luxurious cashmeres, end-of-line vintage silks, jersey knits, herringbone, houndstooth and pinstripe into modern classic pieces, attentive to their past but bursting to belong to the future.

De Castro and Ricci describe their outlook: 'In an industry which is increasingly overproducing, very little is being done to highlight how much is discarded at source, and yet what is being thrown is often intact, still beautiful, and still useable if thought of in a different way.' In 1999, high-street giant Jigsaw introduced the label's signature pieces into its London stores. The relationship developed into a collaboration in which From Somewhere customized and recuperated Jigsaw's unsold and damaged knitwear, effectively reintroducing the company's discarded garments into the market.

Orsola de Castro and Filippo Ricci are the founders and curators of the British Fashion Council Estethica show at London Fashion Week. Ricci also curates Slowhite at the White trade show in Milan, while De Castro is a regular lecturer at sustainable conferences and universities. The line is available from their boutique in London and online through their website.

Patched, pieced, appliquéd and applied, contrasting
fabrics typify From Somewhere's joyful and playful
collection of one-off pieces.

GEOFFREY B. SMALL

A pioneer in avant-garde design and handmade clothing for both women and men, Geoffrey B. Small has shown more collections during Paris Fashion Week than any other American designer. He started his first small business using an old Singer sewing machine in his parent's attic to make clothes for his friends. Within a few years, Small had become Boston's leading bespoke tailor, designing and making clothes for politicians and celebrities alike.

After taking his work to Paris in a suitcase, he showcased his second collection at the Paris sur Mode salon, alongside the likes of Maurizio Altieri and Roberto Cavalli. Cofounder of Yves Saint Laurent and then Chambre Syndicale president Pierre Bergé hailed Small in the pages of *Women's Wear Daily* as one of the few American designers with 'true talent'. Small is only the third American designer to be officially recognized and listed on the calendar of the Chambre Syndicale, France's governing body of haute couture fashion. His controversial first runway collection garnered major press coverage in such industry staples as *Collezioni Trends* magazine, as well as orders from Barneys New York, Charles Gallay in Los Angeles, Maria Luisa in Paris and Albert Eickhoff in Germany.

With Martin Margiela and Xuly Bët, Small is accredited with pioneering the use of recycled design in fashion. At the time considered radical, Small introduced his first recycled menswear collection in Paris in 1996, selling from Paris to Japan in over 40 cities. Counting Winona Ryder, Halle Berry, Tori Spelling and Mariah Carey as clients for his womenswear collection, Small has produced and distributed over 30,000 handmade recycled pieces from his company in Boston.

In the midst of a climate of change in the industry, with many major independent designers forming alliances with large →

Limited-edition, hand-dyed, recycled and reused vintage fabrications are masterfully refashioned into a collection that carries Geoffrey B. Small's social and ethical message.

The limited-edition 'Schola' collection, which carried a warning message against illiteracy, featured models carrying controversial books on ecological and other ethical topics.

corporate global brands, Small made the move to Italy in 1999 and entered into a licensing agreement to produce, finance and distribute his designs. After a few years and reorganized as an independent firm again, he is now making special clothes by hand in his apartment in Italy, in a strictly limited-edition series for a select group of leading stores around the world. With a maximum of 500 pieces per season, Small has survived the ongoing world political and economic crises and continues to produce and develop a pure research collection. He explains, 'Fashion is an art and must be used to raise design quality, not lower it, speak the truth about the world, not lie about it, and do its best to make life better for everyone, not just an elite few.'

His continuously controversial collections address timely social and political messages, such as global feudalism and women in power in the twenty-first century. Small was the first designer at the Paris couture level to introduce designs that specifically addressed global warming and climate change. Presenting his 'Do Something' collection in 2008, Small prompted individuals to take personal action to resolve the world's challenging problems. Forecasting the impending world economic crisis, he began to push the concept of 'hyper-quality', the production of bespoke hand-tailored pieces using the world's best Italian luxury fabrics and a vast array of hand detailing. Alongside his social, political and environmental messages, Small creates one of the most sustainable, personal and environmentally sound luxury wardrobe concepts in the world.

The Geoffrey B. Small line is sold to an exclusive range of high-end boutiques around the world, including the UK, the USA, Japan, Germany and Italy. He limits his distribution to 15 dealers for his handmade pieces per season. He has enjoyed extensive media coverage on MTV and in the magazines American *Vogue*, *Numéro Homme* and *Women's Wear Daily*.

'Fashion is an art and must be used to raise design quality, not lower it, speak the truth about the world, not lie about it, and do its best to make life better for everyone, not just an elite few.'

JOSH JAKUS

Producing a wide range of products from recycled felt for the home and accessories market, Josh Jakus, a California-based designer, makes experiential connections between form and function. His company was founded in 2005 as a means of exploring his lifelong interest in the nature of structure, space and materials through design practice. Driven by intellectual curiosity, Jakus creates a highly innovative collection of purses and handbags, named the UM bags, and made from two layers of factory-excess industrial-wool felt.

Originally inspired by the 1920s Goode Homolosine projection of the world – otherwise known as the 'orange-peel map' due to its resemblance to a flattened hand-peeled rind – Jakus cut a similar shape from recycled felt in the hope that it would form a globe. It did not, but with a continuous zipper to join the edges together, he devised instead his first change purse.

The architectural and sculptural shapes of Jakus's line have a minimal simplicity that belies the complexity of the design, and is heightened by the industrial grey colour of the recycled material. Each purse or bag has brightly contrasting zips and lies completely flat for dry cleaning, storage or travel. The items are developed from two creative challenges: to make use of the density, texture, pliability and strength of pressed-wool felt, and to transform a flat surface into one of volume using only the simplest of operations. These challenges turned out to be mutually beneficial, as Jakus explains: 'The thickness of the felt makes it difficult to sew together, but attaching a zipper was comparatively easy and offered an excellent mechanism for transforming the shape. From there, it was just a matter of finessing the form to create objects that are as practical as they are pleasing.'

An architect by training, with a Master's degree from the University of California, Berkeley, Jakus uses his understanding of the built environment and how it is inhabited to inform his designs, hoping that his products will foster a more intuitive understanding of all objects in the people who use them. He is happiest when making things that are meant to be used.

Much like a highly accomplished martial artist, Jakus achieves maximum effect with the least amount of effort, employing a rigorous design efficiency. He uses materials in their simplest form so that their intrinsic qualities are shown to their best advantage.

The UM bags are available at museum stores, boutiques and design stores across the USA, Australia, Canada, much of Europe, Russia, Singapore and Japan. Jakus's work is also available through online retailers and has been featured in the magazines *Blueprint*, *Scoop Australia*, *Elle*, *Metropolis* and *Casa D*.

'The thickness of the felt makes it difficult to sew together, but attaching a zipper was comparatively easy and offered an excellent mechanism for transforming the shape.'

Created from recycled industrial felt and formed into architectural, spherical shapes, Josh Jakus's bags unzip to lie totally flat.

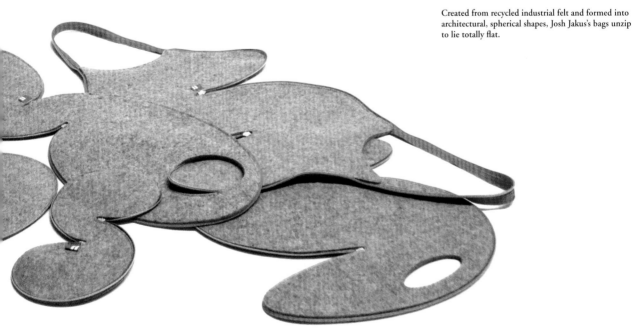

PRELOVED

Preloved creates one-of-a-kind clothing from reclaimed and vintage fabrics: 'Our passion is design and our philosophy is sustainability'. With fit, comfort and style acting as the driving force, the collection is trend-conscious but wearable, with a broad range of items, including dresses, separates and suits. The entire line is beautifully rebuilt out of clothing from the past, including scraps of forgotten work trousers and worn-out curtains that reappear as elegant evening gowns or floaty summer dresses. Subtle layered garments create an easy understated eclecticism, with intriguing mixes of print and solid fabrics juxtaposed to create new harmonies. A playful sophistication permeates the line. Preloved clothes are highly identifiable, while still being individual.

Julia Grieve, the founder, and Peter Friesen, the creative director, have built a celebrity list of devotees that include Hillary Duff, Anne Hathaway and Kate Hudson, to name just a few. A former model, fashion magazine editor and frequent TV guest on Canadian stations, she is in fact a local celebrity herself. She conveyed her own sense of style and her acute design eye and sensitivity to trends through her commentary for the *National Post*'s fashion section.

Grieve's love of recycled clothing began while travelling around the globe as a model, when she would creatively alter and redesign her own clothes, receiving countless compliments on her style. After the completion of her modelling career in 1994, she returned to Toronto and decided to continue her career in the fashion industry, while satisfying a gap in the market by remaking vintage and discarded clothing and materials.

Creative director Peter Friesen was born into a Mennonite family in Paraguay. He moved to Toronto to study fashion design at Ryerson University. An intern at Preloved during his studies, he went on to become creative director on completion of his degree. His role is to design and conceive the collection from concept and theme to finished garment, with Grieve acting as editor or internal buyer, selecting the final pieces to best work in the retail environment.

Preloved now produces a childrenswear collection, as well as a home collection and an accessories line. There are three stand-alone Preloved stores, one in Toronto, another in Montreal and the third in Sydney, Australia. The brand also sells at wholesale worldwide to boutiques in North America, Australia, Europe and Japan, and online. Preloved has received coverage in a number of international fashion magazines, including *Elle*, *Nylon*, *Flair* and *Paper*.

Preloved refashion reclaimed vintage fabrics into
one-of-a-kind clothing with, for example, scraps of
unwanted sweaters and jumpers reappearing as quirky,
patchworked cardigans.

'Our passion is design and our
philosophy is sustainability.'

Inspired by the restrictive designs of vintage clothing,
Preloved reclaims forgotten scraps, re-birthing them
into highly identifiable, unique styles.

REBOUND DESIGNS

Rebound Designs offers a wonderfully innovative collection of handmade bags created out of discarded, recycled, broken and worn vintage hardback books. Each bag is individually handcrafted, taking approximately eight to ten hours to produce, not including the time spent sourcing the books themselves or the trimmings. Fabric for the sides of the bag and the lining is hand-picked to complement the book cover, making each book unique. Caitlin Phillips, the founder of the company, explains, 'I select each lining fabric individually for each cover, to match not only in colour, but whenever possible also in theme, pattern, time period etc. My goal is to choose a fabric that looks as if it grew out of the book.'

Phillips only uses 100 per cent cotton quilting fabric for the lining, a preference she inherited from her mother's love of quilting. Chunky colourful beads form the old-fashioned handle arch. Spots, marks and bent corners are considered part of the book's character and an indicator of its past life; Phillips refers to them as love marks as opposed to scars.

The character and history of each book is left intact, so the precious nature of a well-loved object remains in the bag. Book covers range from full-colour *Alice in Wonderland* titles and children's books to murder mysteries and medical dictionaries in leather and gold leaf, each cover making a distinctive statement. The coverless pages are stored and donated to collage and multimedia artists, as well as to jewellery designers. Phillips herself has started working on various origami projects with the pages, but she is also happy to provide the removed pages along with any bag purchase and at no extra cost.

The idea to make the bags came from seeing purses made from cigar boxes, juice cartons and car number plates, combined with Phillip's love of books. She has a life-long passion for crafting and a history of 'cutting up old things to turn them into something new'.

Phillips also custom-makes bags from customers' favourite books, or will search for a particular title when requested. The purses need to be cared for as if still a book and although reinforced, they cannot be used for heavy everyday wear, and they must not get wet!

The line of bags has now expanded into 'naughty bits' word brooches: hot little pins, with hot little thoughts. Reminiscent of a serial killer's anonymous cut-and-paste confession note, the brooches display naughty excerpts from some of the trashy romance novels Phillips makes her bags from. Suggestive quotes include 'He kept her pinned' and 'She arched her back', while some are more salacious and romantic.

Based in Washington, DC, Phillips sells the purses at the local historic Eastern Market at weekends, as well as through her website and various other East Coast craft shows. She also sells to boutiques in Australia, Singapore and Japan.

Rebound Designs transforms old, damaged and discarded hardback books into individual, quirky purses with character.

RIEDIZIONI

Riedizioni is the trademark of a series of bags and products for the home and office made from textile waste and leftovers bound together in plastic. It includes a variety of totes, purses, document holders and place mats, each with an alluring combination of yarn, threads and selvedges. Each piece is unique due to the textiles employed and the production process, with a machine deciding what combinations to use in each case. The material has a hybrid organic-synthetic feel, with yarns and selvedges combined into naturalistic patterns or regimented rows. The pieces are encased in rubberized plastic and bear more than a passing resemblance to cryogenics for fabric waste or suspended animation for thread balls. Yet, somehow, these otherwise utterly useless micro-scraps and fabric ends make for extremely pleasing and desirable bags and purses. Shining through their rubbery grave, the discarded scraps of fabric and waste reveal their own unique beauty and value.

As head of research for a major Italian textile company, Luisa Cevese, the designer behind the Riedizioni label, became aware of the amount and consistency of textile waste, which led her to consider the possibility of a design project using scraps as the basic element. Having gained some understanding of the plastics industry, she started to combine textile waste with different types of plastic, as she explains, 'plastic gives our products durability, strength, flexibility, waterproofing and structure'. Seeing such a tremendous opportunity for the development of this new material, which neither a textile nor a plastic company could fully exploit, she decided to take on the challenge herself and founded the company. Cevese describes her approach: 'Opposites meet. Unique and serial. Soft and resistant. Fun and elegant. Modern and classic. Craft and industry.'

The textile industry creates an enormous amount of waste: large blocks of unusable ends, damaged fabric, yarns and threads, selvedges, small uneven pieces of cloth and cuts from garments. Riedizioni recycles both natural and manmade fibres, the only criteria being that the textile must enable them to produce a constant design out of a discontinuous element. Other textile waste used in Riedizioni's bags range from damaged fishermen's nets and discarded kimonos and saris to burlap coffee bags and fur balls. The plastic employed in each item varies based on need and can be hard, soft, thick, thin, matt, transparent, recycled or not. The objective is to find the simplest solution that involves the minimum amount of waste.

Sold across the USA, the UK, Germany, Austria, Italy, France, Japan and Greece at an impressive number of high-end retail outlets, boutiques and museum stores and online, Riedizioni has also been the focus of a number of magazine articles and has been featured in *Textile Designers at the Cutting Edge* by Bradley Quinn.

Riedizioni's bags are made from an innovative material that combines textile scraps with plastic.

'I love waste, working with waste.'

STEPHAN
HANN

Based in Berlin, Stephan Hann is a fashion artist who specializes in recycled couture, reclaiming unwanted and discarded items not usually associated with fashion and reworking them into one-off pieces of wearable art. Surplus champagne bottle caps are connected to form modern-day chain mail; photographic film is woven into lavish and frothy gowns; cartoon-adorned tetrapacks are cut into tiny shapes like fish scales and sewn together to form a dress; and dozens of vintage French military purses, a flea-market find, are refashioned to become a mini skirt. The first impression of the designs often belies the deeper meaning behind them. The French military purses, for example, were the only personal item soldiers could take into battle with them. These lost and forgotten purses each symbolize a lost soul, brought to life again in the reworking of them into a very feminine piece of clothing. Only close inspection of the garments reveals the original nature of the materials.

Hann's working methodology is very tactile, and he begins by establishing a relationship with the material and finding new definitions for the raw materials. His motivation is always the individual material find. The establishment of this process was initially due to financial constraints, but now persists as a preference. Friends originally donated items to him, but as his popularity grew he started collecting things himself by haunting Paris's flea markets. Interested in the 'visual possibilities' of the fabrics, he uses recycling as a means of reminiscence, conservation and a way of preserving the memory of trivial materials and altering their context by turning them into valued items of art by ennobling them through his couture workmanship. →

A fashion artist, Stephan Hann creates visual possibilities in three-dimensional form with materials not usually associated with fashion, such as celluloid film skilfully combined to form frothy loops or paper folded into tiny plissée pieces.

Working with retired seamstresses from the Berlin German Opera, Hann handcrafts each item in its entirety, relying heavily on the wealth of experience in his aging team of workers that makes many of his structures possible.

Trained as a menswear bespoke tailor at the Berlin German Opera prior to attending The School of Art and Design in Berlin where he studied costume and stage design, Hann undertook an internship in the costume workshop at the Berlin Theatre, where he learned his respect for craft and the couture approach of handcrafting individual items. On graduation, he went on to collaborate with Loulou de la Falaise, long-time assistant to Yves Saint Laurent, and has since worked for the fashion house of Swarovski where his mandate was to find new materials and combinations, working with plastics, leather and latex to produce a highly exclusive collection of purses and cashmere pullovers. Hann's creations are sometimes the result of commissions – for example, for Moët & Chandon and Lexmark papers – and other times the result of specific exhibition requests, for such organizations as the Netherlands Architectural Institute (NAi) in Rotterdam and the German National Museum in Nuremberg.

Consulting for German TV telenovela (a television serial drama) *Sophie*, Hann has also designed costumes for the Stuttgart Opera and has exhibited his 'Recycling Couture' in many exhibitions from Germany and Paris to Moscow.

SUITCASE

Growing up in Brazil, with a culture of recycling as a necessity rather than a philosophy, Edson Raupp learned to value recycling products and materials. He explains: 'Being part of large family where resources were limited, it was always necessary to consider reusing products and materials.'

Encouraged at school to be resourceful as well as ecologically sound, Raupp made inventive products for the local market, such as shoe-cleaning mats made from the metal caps of fizzy-drink bottles and rugs made from scraps from his father's tailoring business. Raupp elaborates: 'The ecologically sound aspect of this did not so much come from a highly developed philosophical or political position, but rather because reusing and saving was natural behaviour based on good sense, good economics and the dislike of waste.'

Raupp grew up helping his father with small tasks, learning how to sew and to understand construction along the way. Experimenting with the techniques his father taught him, he made dressing-up costumes for himself and his sister by sewing tree leaves together with needles made from orange-tree thorns. While studying fine arts at university, he continued this trend of recycling and reusing by making a line of jewellery from leftover plastic cutlery and paper plates from campus parties.

Later in the UK, when Raupp was considering starting his own business, he naturally turned to men's suits and recycling for his inspiration. Starting with a reversal of the work his father so painstakingly undertook, he deconstructed men's suit jackets, only to reconstruct them in different forms, which as Raupp says, 'probably explains why the finished product, although obviously mixed-up also appears tailored'.

His first experiment in making a bag from an old suit elicited such a response from his friends that he was encouraged to continue. Over a short period of time, Raupp developed and refined a unique collection of bag styles, all made from recycled men's suit jackets salvaged from charity shops in the UK, and selling under the Suitcase label. Each jacket is individually cut to optimize its characteristic shape, design and colour, producing an eccentric, quirky bag from sleeves, pockets and lapels.

Shoulder straps are fashioned from discarded car-seat webbing and measuring tapes. Raupp designs and makes each of the bags in the collection himself, as he says, the work 'cannot be done by using a template as the structure of each jacket is different and the details vary in proportion and style'.

Having exhausted his experimentation with men's suits made into bags, Raupp has expanded his line to include bag designs made from garment labels and buttons, all equally inventive and beautiful.

Selling first at Camden Market and Covent Garden craft market in London, Raupp then showed at different craft fairs. From contacts made at the fairs, he went on to exhibit his work at various galleries. He now sells to the Victoria & Albert Museum shop and the Contemporary Applied Arts Gallery in London, but also to shops in Tokyo, Hong Kong, Paris, Hamburg and Sydney and online.

135 RECYCLE, REUSE & REDESIGN

Suitcase transforms all the classic elements of an
English gentleman's suit jacket into bag designs.

TRAIDREMADE

A recycled fashion label, TRAIDremade provides a stylish alternative to high-street fashion. Founded in 2000, TRAIDremade's designers mix, match, rip, cut, sew and print torn and stained clothing to reproduce high-street fashion trends exclusively out of donated materials that come from TRAID's 900 textile recycling banks across the UK. The bulk of the donations is sold through the company's nine charity shops, while TRAIDremade was conceived when staff recognized the waste created by donated damaged clothing. Torn and stained donations are saved from landfill and redesigned and reconstructed into completely unique and original pieces to be sold under the TRAIDremade label. Creating quirky eclectic fashions with a touch of glamour and a retro feel, TRAIDremade's team of designers, headed by Paula Kirkwood, produce one-off pieces for discerning fashion-conscious individuals. The money raised by TRAID is used to expand its recycling activities, fund workshops in London schools and is donated to overseas development projects.

TRAID stands for Textile Recycling for Aid and International Development. As a registered charity, it aims to protect the environment by diverting clothes and shoes from landfill, reduce world poverty by raising funds for overseas development projects and educate the public on environmental and world poverty issues. Since TRAID's launch, it has donated over £1.2 million (US$1.8 million) to bring real improvements to the lives of people in some of the poorest regions of the world. Projects have included increasing the supply of clean water in villages in Kenya, enabling people affected by HIV to run their own micro-solar businesses in Malawi and creating a fishing cooperative in the Philippines.

In 2002, TRAID brought second-hand and recycled clothing to the mainstream through a partnership with high-street chain Topman, who bought vintage and customized clothing from TRAID to sell through its Oxford Circus store. As the charity states: 'The problems with cheap chic and throwaway fashion are complex. There are already hundreds of millions of items of clothing that are being thrown away year after year in the UK. Much of the older clothing is of high quality and very durable. Why not reuse this clothing again and again?'

TRAID also runs regular office events across London, known as 'Suit into Loot', offering busy professionals the chance to clear out their wardrobes and make a positive contribution towards the environment and the world's poor. Employees are given easy-to-carry environmentally friendly jute bags to bring their unwanted suits into work, with Loot staff collecting the donations for TRAID and resale.

Additionally, TRAID's education arm offers a variety of activities where students are encouraged to explore and discuss contemporary and relevant topics including waste, reuse and recycling, climate change, ethical fashion and world poverty. Students at primary as well as university level are given an overview of TRAID and its work, as well as a demonstration of TRAIDremade.

Using damaged and stained clothing, TRAIDremade reconfigures discarded gems into one-off designs by patching, piecing and printing.

TRAIDremade work exclusively with donated clothing
and textiles that have been diverted from landfills,
with every garment sold to help support international
development projects that fight poverty.

Chapter Four
NEW MODELS

We are in the midst of a major shift in world view, a cultural shift that brings into the mainstream ecological and social consciousness. The major motivation for this global movement is the need to take personal responsibility for ecological and social change in the midst of global warming and climate crisis. The high-profile exposure of the ecological state of the planet, once so hotly debated and denied by governments and scientists worldwide but no longer in question, is the major reason that ecology- and social-outreach fashion-design companies now cover all areas of design. Educator and activist Parker Palmer explains: 'Movements begin when people refuse to live divided lives. This is what is happening with the cultural creatives, many of whom are going through major life transitions as they look for ways to live the values they have come to believe in.'

The term 'cultural creative' was coined by Paul Ray and Sherry Ruth Anderson in their seminal book *The Cultural Creatives: How 50 Million People are Changing the World*, which documents the predominately creatively led movement that is forging a shift in world view towards a more ethical and ecological future in all aspects of life, including business. According to their statistics, the cultural creatives constitute 26 per cent of the American population, some 50 million people, with a further 80 to 90 million people across Europe. They affect the ways in which people do business and act as the driving force behind the demand that we go beyond environmental regulation to ensure substantive ecological change.

Books such as *The Cultural Creatives*, *Cradle to Cradle* by Michael Braungart and William McDonough and the *The Rise of the Creative Class* by Richard Florida, to mention just a few, have all documented this shift in world view. Hence, the broad range of companies now having an impact on production and consumption across different fields.

Artistic expression, both commercial and non-commercial, has always played a part in informing and expressing shifts in cultural viewpoint and imagining new futures, both good and bad. Fashion, as part of commercial art, is perhaps not the most obvious arena in which to forge a new future or to make a political or social statement. Nevertheless, a range of socially and ecologically aware fashion designers has emerged. Indeed, some companies are challenging how business itself is conducted, not just with a view to their product, but encompassing their entire structural model. Commerce, as a general rule, tends to follow well-established methodologies, with minimal changes applied to sourcing, production and logistics since mass production began. Anyone questioning the conventional method of doing business is making a radical statement. Yet companies such as Nau in Portland, Oregon, for example, use their business model to question every accepted notion of how and why things are done, more often than not finding alternative means of achieving the same or better end results. Individual researchers have managed to fuse nature and technology to produce highly innovative means of renewing products rather than making entirely new ones, for example, Rebecca Earley's 'Twice Upcycled Shirt' collection. Others, such as Holly McQuillan, envisage completely new ways of designing and cutting garments to eliminate waste, a complete departure from the standard patternmaking used in the industry.

As Albert Einstein said, 'We cannot solve the problems we have created with the same thinking that created them.'

cled' polyester shirts by
photogram printing to give

AFOREST-DESIGN

A unique Internet-based design company, aforest-design was launched in 2003 by Sara Lamúrias. A Portuguese project, born of a desire to communicate ideas through art, design and fashion, it creates products and organizes events with a highly artistic focus. aforest design and develop limited-edition or made-to-order products that carry a personality of their own. Eclectic and artistic product lines include silk-screened sweaters, handmade and handwritten message bracelets for special friends, artists' paint-palette T-shirts made in collaboration with contemporary fine artists in the colours of their current works and exquisite photographically printed tabi socks. On top of this, aforest also produces a full coordinating collection of cotton separates.

The brand is all about collaboration, with designers and artists working together on small projects and collections that come about through happenstance and a process of connection and identification, culminating in an invitation to work together on a project, with royalties and promotion as the trade-off. Lamúrias explains, 'The aforest brand stands for passion, for small and big-time events. Artists and dreamers who are politically or socially aware. For juveniles, no matter what age.' aforest also supports artistic and intellectual movements and causes through the creation of product lines and promotions; for example, for the 'TV Off' movement, aforest developed a series of tongue-in-cheek knitted accessories, intended to get people questioning the role of TV in their lives.

Values and passions, learning and teaching, growth and change are all topics that aforest explores. The company has expanded from producing made-to-order items to larger collections that show at Lisbon Fashion Week and other international fairs. Like other artist-led brands, however, aforest has chosen to limit its expansion to ensure a base of strong products rather than big collections. They will not allow the market to define their format, scale or products, preferring to be involved with artistic exhibitions and small-scale projects. As Lamúrias states, 'This is something important about aforest: it's not a limited brand defined by a market, it's free to say what it believes in.'

As a small company with small production, it is often difficult for aforest to buy the minimums imposed by the industry, so it looks for alternatives that are achievable at its scale, as well as sustainable for the company and the environment. This has led them to work on a collaboration with female inmates at the Estabelecimento Prisional de Tires in Cascais, where the prisoners make accessories for the collection in return for pay. Teaching the inmates new techniques and marketable skills, the project also supplies them with stimulating and interesting work.

aforest offset their carbon emissions through a tree-planting project in their chosen forest. Lamúrias describes her design philosophy: 'If I can make someone happier when I'm producing, I do it. If I can't buy a more ecological material, then I find a way to translate it into something good. If I can say through my products or events that some social phenomenon is important to pay attention to, I do.'

A unique collaboration of artists and designers, aforest-design create unique products in limited editions to communicate ideas through art, design and fashion.

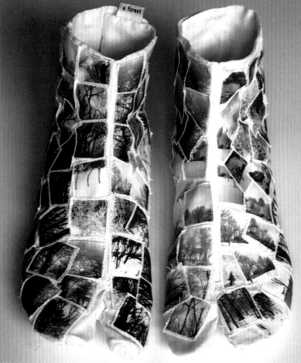

aforest's stop motion collection is a sequence of graphically printed and linked garments based on the animation technique that makes static objects move.

The odori tabi socks are limited-edition traditional Japanese-style socks, featuring five different photographically printed nature themes.

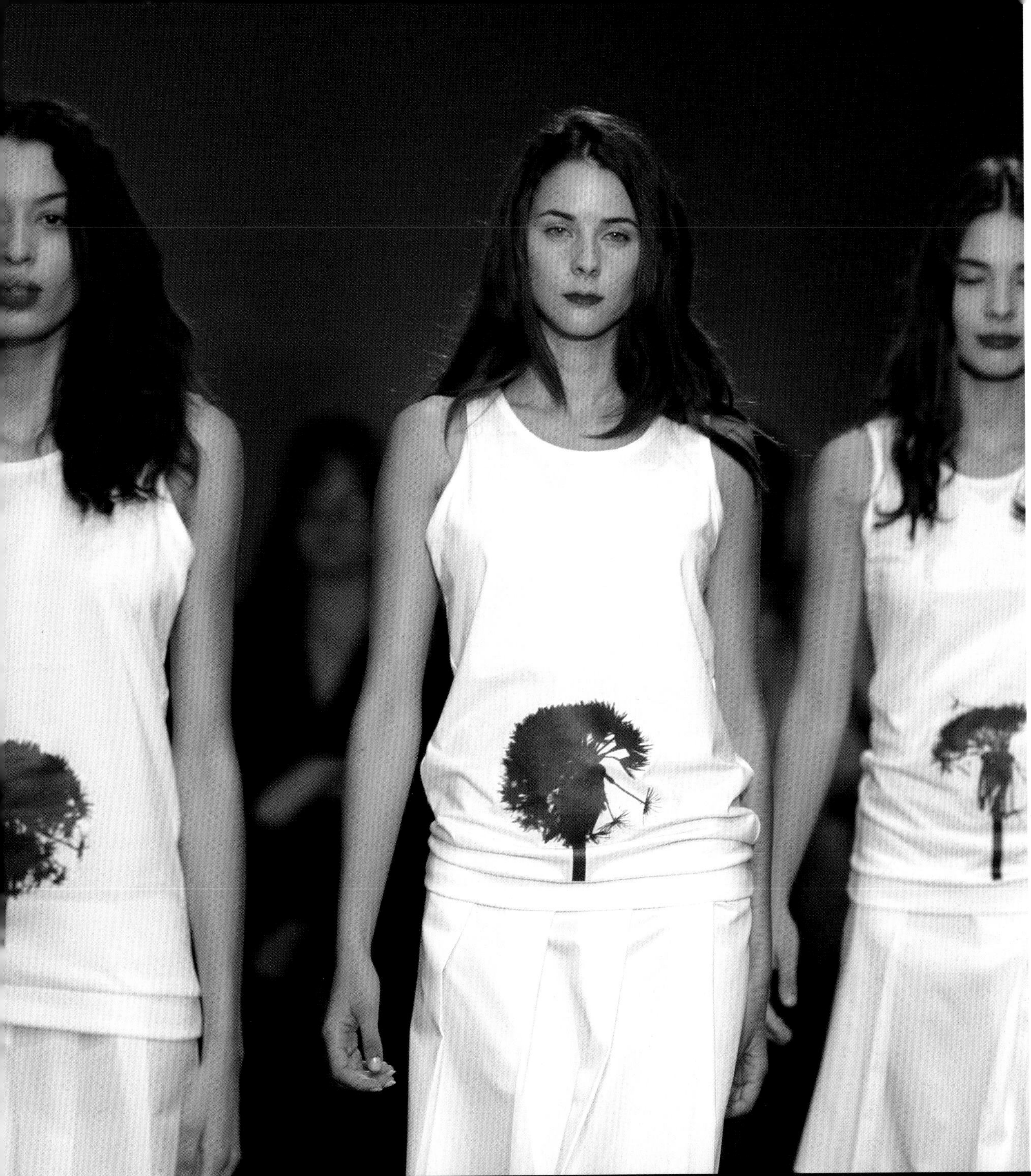

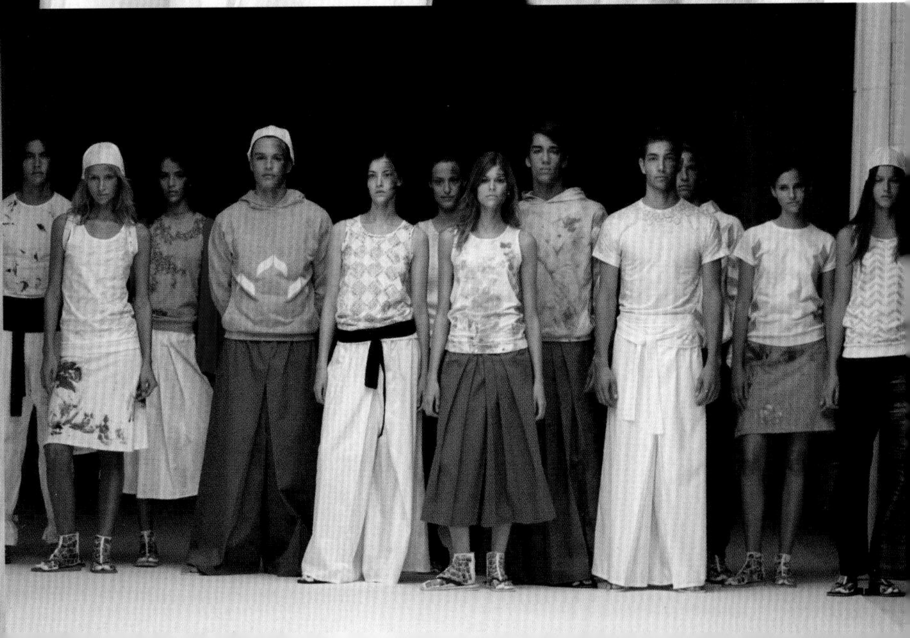

ANDREA ZITTEL

Andrea Zittel is a California-based sculptor and installation artist, whose work is an ongoing experiment and exploration in living as it relates to shelter, food, furniture and clothing, and is in response to her daily routines and surroundings. In the early 1990s, as a young artist with very little money and working in an office job where she was expected to wear 'something respectable', Zittel conceived the 'Uniform Project'. Now her longest-running art project, it started as a pragmatic response to her situation, while at the same time confronting the values placed on fashion. Each season, Zittel designed one perfect black dress, had it made by a professional seamstress to her specifications and wore it every day for an entire season. The project evolved over the years to explore her changing interests, moving from the perfect black dress to an exploration of Russian constructivism, working only with rectangles of fabric that she could sew herself. Simplifying the concept over time, Zittel used rectangles of fabric literally torn from the bolt of fabric, then moved on to crocheted dresses formed from a single continuous thread until, finally, she eliminated even the crochet hook and manipulated the strands of thread with her fingers. Then, in 2002, she discovered felting: 'Now I am finally beginning to make the most direct form of clothing possible by hand-felting wool directly into the shape of a garment.'

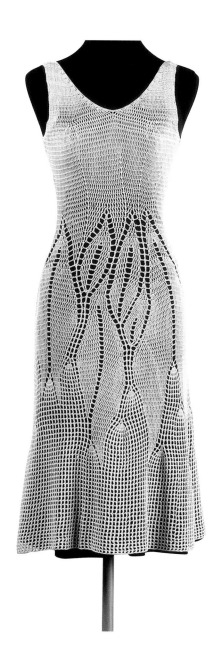

Fascinated by the flexibility of felting, Zittel creates seamless dresses formed directly in three dimensions. Quickly exceeding her strict seasonal requirements, she produces variations in colour, texture, thickness and ornamentation. Creating exquisite pieces with simple silhouettes, she highlights the uniqueness of the material by incorporating dripping hems and lava-lamp-like holes. Each piece is imbued with a sense of organic connection to the material itself, as if it were made from wood or stone.

Zittel also founded the 'smockshop', an artist-run enterprise that generates income for artists whose work is either non-commercial or not yet self-sustaining. The 'smock', designed by Zittel, is a simple wraparound garment sewn by the artists themselves, using their own artistic interpretation, to create one-of-a-kind pieces. Sales of the smocks generate income and provide artists with alternative space for experimental works on parcels of land located along a stretch of desert community encompassing the Joshua Tree.

Graduating with a degree in painting and sculpture from San Diego State University and a Master's in sculpture from the Rhode Island School of Design, Zittel has featured in countless joint and solo exhibitions around the world. In the USA, her work has appeared at the Whitney Museum of American Art, the Smithsonian Institution, the Museum of Modern Art in New York and the Guggenheim Museum. She teaches at the Roski School of Fine Arts at the University of Southern California, where she commutes between the desert and California.

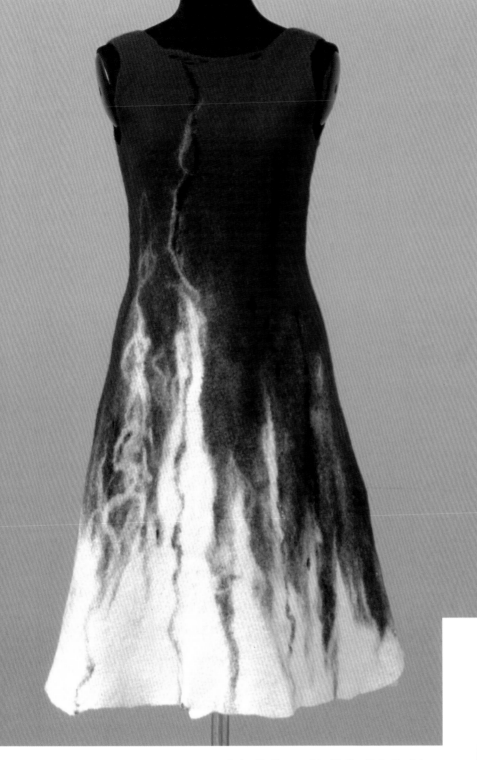

Andrea Zittel's ever-evolving 'Uniform Project' has led to the exploration of material and form in relationship to her social environment, and developed it into one fabulous outfit per season.

Crocheted, felted and smocked dresses are just some of
the end results of Zittel's explorations of clothing and
the environment.

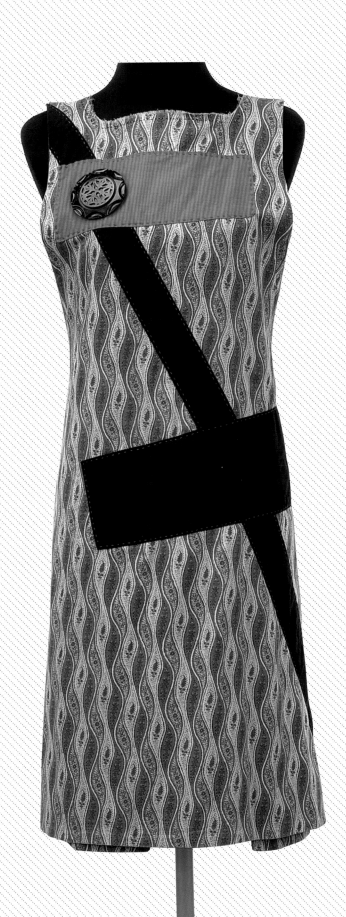

BLESS

Desiree Heiss and Ines Kaag, founders of Bless, met as students in Paris. A scant three years later, Bless was born. The label produces a wide range of products, including fashion clothing, accessories, home décor and some objects that defy categorization. Featuring such unforgettable items as cable jewellery for decorating computer wires, a limited edition of fur wigs, disposable T-shirts and an assortment of clothing items guaranteed to 'fuck up every style', Bless also sells a range of found objects and has teamed up for joint projects with Adidas on sneakers and Bucherer on jewellery. The designers explain, 'Bless is a project that presents ideal and artistic values through products to the public.'

The original concept behind Bless was to distil down each collection to a single numbered item. Realizing that this pure minimal idea was not as financially viable as it was ecologically sound, Bless expanded the collection, which has now grown to number 35. The designers still prefer to work outside the usual model of seasonal collections, which they find boring. They do not consider themselves artists, shying away from the rarified atmosphere of the art gallery, which they feel is stagnant, preferring instead to produce useful functional items based on their own needs and those of their partners, co-workers and friends. Clearly, however, they do not fall into the traditional fashion-design category either, choosing to call themselves simply designers. They state, 'Bless is a visionary substitute to make the near future worth living for.'

Of German origin, the company now has stores, also identified by number, across Europe and has participated in a multitude of collaborations and exhibitions globally. Blessed with what seems to be an unending source of ideas, they have produced some ingenious concepts. One such idea is Bless No 20, which is an attempt to respond to the traveller's eternal problem of heavy luggage and to extend possible hotel services to enhance the client's comfort during his or her stay. The hotel guest finds in his or her hotel wardrobe a small selection of basic and useful clothes, such as underwear, a knitted sweater, a suit, a dress, sunglasses, a bag and other items for his or her disposal during their stay. Ideally, this hotel service functions as both a useful wardrobe supplement and a refreshing discovery of an alternative approach to design.

The Bless team often finds interesting objects in charity shops and other retailers, which, with a deep appreciation of good design, they revalue by reselling them through high-end stores such as Colette in Paris, which they feel is a more appropriate setting for the previously undervalued product. The designers do not put their own label on the found objects, but 'escort' each item with a postcard instead. One of the items they have revalued under Bless No 8 is a collection of leather socks originally intended as footwear for the mosque and available in a rainbow of colours. Others have included low-end mass-market designs, which Bless simply felt were underappreciated. These items are perfect exactly as they are, hence the designers' insistence not to use them as sources of inspiration for their own collection, but simply to expose them to a different audience without adulteration on their part.

Bless investigate the boundaries of style through clothing design, creating themeless items based on need and purpose.

COLLECTION
OF HOPE

'Collection of Hope' was created as part of a workshop by second-year students at the ESMOD Berlin and Munich fashion schools. On a trip to Kenya, the ESMOD faculty, representatives from Galeries Lafayette, i-magine (the German AIDS awareness foundation) and former model Waridi Schrobsdorff visited the Amani self-help community in Sultan Hamud, near the capital Nairobi. The community is home to 70 children aged between 2 months and 17 years, many HIV positive, and 28 HIV-positive adults, all supported by i-magine.

Inspired by the country, its culture and, of course, the people, the idea was born to build a project based on exchange between the two cultures. Returning to Berlin and Munich full of inspiration, the ESMOD faculty began their second-year student coursework with a workshop on Africa and social responsibility, discussing the aesthetics, sense, sensuality and social, cultural and economic significance of textiles and clothing in modern Africa.

With this in mind, the students developed individual collections that respected sustainability and fair trade. On completion, a jury made up of retailers, designers and PR agencies selected the strongest pieces, which went on to form a final collection. In addition to the clothing, the logo and accompanying corporate designs were also based on marketing concepts conceived by the students. The result is a womenswear collection comprising 30 pieces and a children's collection of 10 pieces, all made exclusively from eco-materials. The students explain their thought process: 'Let's make a collection together. Let's go further and set up an independent company, which both the helpers and the supported profit from. A collection to inspire hope. The Collection of Hope.'

'With the "Collection of Hope", we would like to show people in Europe a whole new side to Africa,' explains Waridi Schrobsdorff. It was important that the project should be profitable for both sides: the students are provided with a platform on which to present their work and their names appear on their pieces, while 50 per cent of the net profit goes directly to the Amani self-help group to provide children in Africa with a proper education. The hope is that once the project is established some of the production will move to Sultan Hamud. More cooperation projects are planned for the future to secure the continuing development of the enterprise.

Showing at multiple trade shows, exhibitions and catwalk shows around the world, including Bread & Butter Barcelona and Mercedes-Benz Fashion Week Berlin, the collection is for sale in Galeries Lafayette in Berlin as well as in other stores across Germany, and through their own website. The 'Collection of Hope' line is presented twice a year and made entirely in Germany.

This photo-printed T-shirt, with head-wrap and outsized African print jewellery, is designed by students at the ESMOD fashion school in Germany. This and other designs by 'Collection of Hope' are produced for the benefit of the Amani self-help group in Kenya.

HOLLY MCQUILLAN

Holly McQuillan has been making her own clothes since she was eight. It was not until she was at Inglewood High School in Taranaki, New Zealand, however, that she realized fashion could be more than a hobby. Now a design lecturer and practitioner within what she calls 'the often hideous but always exciting world of fashion', she is intent on 'saving the world one frock at a time'. She says, 'I love fashion! It is beautiful, frightening, exhilarating, confronting, elegant, communicative, intelligent, frivolous and thought provoking.'

However, as an ecologically and socially conscious individual, McQuillan is far more aware than your average fashionista that fashion is the cause of massive environmental and social injustice. Sustainable fashion remains an oxymoron to McQuillan, after all, 'How can an industry be considered sustainable when its primary concern is the propagation of the next new thing at the expense of perfectly functional existing products?'

Concerned that the fashion industry is responding to climate crisis with what she terms 'less bad' solutions, i.e. using organic and recycled fibres but within a wasteful production and consumption model. The industry norm is 15 per cent textile waste generated through production; that is 15 per cent of all textiles purchased for garment production are destined for the bin, resulting in loss of profit for the manufacturer, but also enormous quantities of textile waste destined for landfill. Add the fact that most garments travel enormous distances from the cotton field to the consumer – with raw fibre sourced in one country, finishing done in another, weaving in yet another, cutting and making in another – and your average garment racks up considerable mileage and hence generates vast quantities of carbon dioxide. This has led to the development of McQuillan's unique design and cutting process that totally eliminates textile waste. All the parts that are removed for fit or aesthetic reasons are reincorporated back into the garment. Surplus becomes a resource, not to be used for another product at some time in the future but as a resource for its own creation.

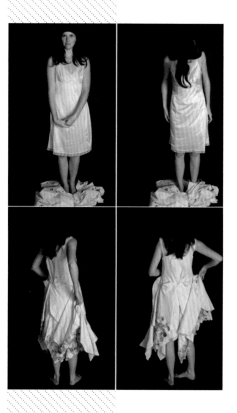

For McQuillan, the conflict is what she terms 'triadic'; she envisions herself 'sitting on the very pointy apex of a three-sided pyramid' made up of sustainable designer, educator and fashion lover, creating a very delicate balance between the three. Conflicting with her role as an educator – teaching others how to create new products – she struggles with her knowledge of what damage consumption has already done and continues to do to the planet. This has led to a precarious balancing act for McQuillan and the realization that uncertainty can be a great innovator. 'The driving force of my design practice is the embracing and development of an ease of risk while designing. I feel that when designing for an uncertain world, it could make sense to use a process that mimics the level of risk inherent in living on our planet.'

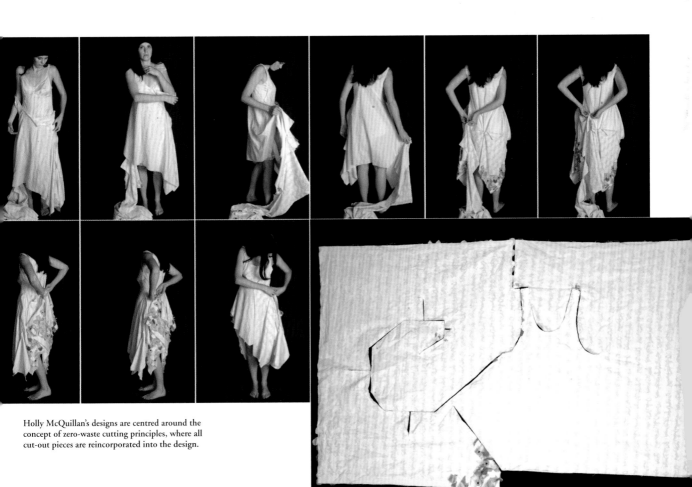

Holly McQuillan's designs are centred around the concept of zero-waste cutting principles, where all cut-out pieces are reincorporated into the design.

Digital printing is configured into highly complex
designs that incorporate all waste into the design itself
in Holly McQuillan's work.

MARK LIU

Based in London, Mark Liu graduated from the University of Technology in Sydney, Australia with a degree in The Implications of Nanotechnology Textiles on Fashion Products and Lifestyle Trends. After graduating, Liu was accepted into Central Saint Martins for his MA, where he pursued research into nanotechnology textiles, with internships at Alexander McQueen, Miss Selfridge and Ghost.

His 'Zero Waste' collection, launched in 2007, broke ground in eco-consciousness by engineering every item in the collection from single rectangles of fabric and incorporating highly complex and detailed pattern cutting to make each pattern piece fit together like an ornate jigsaw puzzle, thereby completely eliminating material waste. Generally, 15 per cent of fabric is wasted in the cutting process of an average garment, and this was the inspiration behind the ingenuity of his cutting technique. The jigsaw of interlocking pattern pieces translates into garments that are engineered to the extreme. Liu is motivated by his passion for eco-sustainability and his desire to push the boundaries of fashion through innovative design. He explains, 'Wasted materials are bad for the environment and a loss in potential profits.'

The 'Zero Waste' collection was Liu's graduating thesis. Selected as one of Australia's 17 upcoming designers at Sydney Design Week, Liu's collection toured the Chinese cities of Shanghai, Guangzhou and Chongqing for the exhibition Climate Cool by Design. He went on to exhibit his first professional collection, 'On the Cutting Edge' at the Estethica show during London Fashion Week.

Reminiscent of Zandra Rhodes in the intricacy of his textile designs and in the way that the textile informs and dictates the cut of the garment, Liu creates pieces that are elaborate and three-dimensional. His prints are inspired by the similarity between sword intaglio designs and lace patterns. Using mainly silk and wools, Liu experiments with eco-friendly materials and pigments. Each design is painstakingly cut out by hand with scissors, 'confidence and patience'. Sometimes the edges are heat-sealed to stop fraying. As Liu says, 'It's all about taking yourself out of the your comfort zone and doing what you believe in instead of simply what is easy. Sometimes the more you risk, the more you stand to gain.' →

Incredibly complex prints and cut-out shapes are pieced together to create intricate feathered styling and layering in Mark Liu's handmade garments.

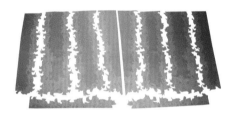

Even complex digital print designs for these dresses, with their intricate styling, are conceived with Liu's zero-waste policy.

Collections invariably have an intellectual theme as Liu loves the concept of brinksmanship and consistently uses it to inform his work. His 'Rogue Agent' collection questions whether it is possible for an individual to make a difference against an established system. It directly challenges the fashion system with the realization that wasteful and unethical behaviour is built into its very thought process. He comes to the conclusion that to confront the problems all previous assumptions have to be abandoned and the rules broken, cheated or subverted.

His Autumn/Winter 09/10 collection is inspired by a phenomenon called the 'Singularity Point', which is the moment when a system becomes aware of its own limitations and eventually rewrites its own rules to take control of its own destiny. Liu elaborates, 'I have applied this principle to the fashion system to make environmentally friendly changes through innovations in tailoring and textiles. Some of the changes were so dramatic that most of the garments in the collection were constructed without even using a sewing machine.'

Liu envisions a future where sustainability will promote innovation in fashion as well as new aesthetics in style.

NAU

Translated from Maori and meaning 'welcome, come in', Nau is a design-oriented performance sportswear company that is breaking the model of how fashion companies do business. Nau's goal is to demonstrate the highest levels of citizenship in everything they do, from product development to production and from labour and environmental practices to philanthropy. For Nau, companies have a broader responsibility than simply generating profit: 'We're a small group of people, committed to the power of business as a force for change. Defined by what we love, and how we work and play, we're looking to do more than make clothes; we're seeking to redefine what it means to be successful.'

The company pledges 5 per cent of all sales to a range of charitable organizations dedicated to solving environmental and humanitarian problems. Nau puts the decision of which charity will benefit from individual purchases in the hands of its customers, by prompting them to choose from various 'partners for change'. In under a year of business, they had donated $223,000. Ian Yolles, vice president of marketing, and Chris Van Dyke, CEO, have created a range of web-based venues for telling the stories woven through the company and their employees. Incorporating the interests and passions of their audience and community through the Nau blog, they include documentary-style storytelling showcasing their heroes, the Thought Kitchen, which they describe as their 'first foray into stirring the pot' and their 'partners for change'. The commitment to put the environment, human rights, public health and safety, the communities in which it operates and the dignity of its employees on the same level as those of its shareholders is written into Nau's articles of incorporation. 'We're challenging the nature of capitalism. We believed every single operational element in our business was an opportunity to turn traditional business notions inside out, integrating environmental, social, and economic factors.'

Nau's overlapping customer base of 'multidimensional outdoor athletes', 'new activists' and 'creatives' informs the three elements of Nau's design philosophy: performance, sustainability and beauty. The company resolves to achieve all three in an industry where combining even two of those qualities is rare. 'The challenge for us was to blow up baked-in assumptions: if you have fashion, you can't get performance, or if you want sustainability, it won't be good-looking. It's not about the proliferation of SKUs and feeding the consumer disease. It's about designs that are timeless rather than trend-driven and colors that work over multiple seasons and situations.'

In May of 2008 Nau posted a proud overview of its achievements, concluding the blog with a notice of the closure of their business, citing the crisis in capital markets and their own 'audacity to challenge conventional paradigms of what a business should be'. In less than two months, however, Nau managed to relaunch, albeit without their retail venues, focusing more on e-commerce and existing partnerships. On their blog they state: 'Business can be a force for social and environmental good…We'll continue to act as host for the collective community of like-minded individuals who are committed to positive change and are reflecting this in all aspects of their lives.'

Nau are a small group of people committed to positive change by creating a new model of social entrepreneurship in design by combining performance, sustainability and beauty.

REBECCA EARLEY & KATE GOLDS-WORTHY

Rebecca Earley is a designer and reader at the Textile Environment Design (TED) research lab at Chelsea College of Art & Design in London. Developing a series of upcycled shirts by sourcing 100 discarded blouses from charity shops, Earley reinvents each shirt by reshaping and overprinting them. Upcycling refers to the process of taking a relatively worthless item and investing value into it, making it desirable again. Using heat photogram printing with recycled paper and reactive dyes, stains are covered with photographic prints of natural items such as a real palm leaf. It is not recycling, as it is not merely reusing something, but it is reinventing it, redesigning it or recombining it to give it a whole new life, not a second-hand one.

When the shirt has come to the end of its second life and is once more discarded, it can be returned for its third life as a quilted waistcoat, for which it is recut, lined in recycled polyester fleece and finished. In collaboration with PhD student Kate Goldsworthy, the materials are fused together with a permanent bonding process developed for her PhD research thesis, which is achieved without adhesives or bonding agents. This process of fusing, according to a preset digital pattern, achieves simultaneous surface decoration. Laser-etching creates a delicate lace-like effect, with melted transparent materials digitally controlled without any added agents. The lack of adhesives and additives is a key element of the work, as is making the upcycling process completely out of existing materials not new ones, hence not creating any waste; in fact, the opposite, as it turns waste into something valuable. This small group of triple-upcycled shirts constitutes two collaborative pieces out of the 100. →

'By imagining and designing-in multiple life cycles at the outset, a designer can maximize the potential of "borrowed" materials, which are designed to go back into the melting pot and emerge again when needed.'

Rebecca Earley's upcycling techniques involve reshaping and overprinting polyester shirts using heat photogram printing with low impact dyes and a real palm leaf.

Their work has centred around the concept of upcycling, to reinvigorate and redesign discarded polyester shirts into newly valued and desirable pieces.

Mindful of the impact of textile and clothing production on the environment, Earley developed the twice-upcycled shirt project with polyester shirts, which take more than 200 years to decompose in landfill. The collection addresses ideas about emotionally durable design while using new technologies, with the end intention that the 100 shirts should be exhibited in a combined high-fashion and art environment. The project also explores 'resurfacing' as a means to produce upcycled textile products from low-grade fibre waste, which can be recycled through multiple lifetimes and ultimately presented as a mono-material. The role of the designer in the eyes of Earley and Goldsworthy is to create products that have minimal impact on the environment, based on the concept of life-cycle thinking through design intervention. Earley explains, 'By imagining and designing-in multiple life cycles at the outset, a designer can maximize the potential of "borrowed" materials, which are designed to go back into the melting pot and emerge again when needed.'

The project is concerned with technologies that could change the way we recycle textile waste and the role of the designer in the collaborative redesign process, based on the concept of materials as only 'interim' resources and creating multi-life textiles and garments as the end aim. Goldsworthy's research has drawn upon the theories of *Cradle to Cradle: Remaking the Way We Make Things* by William McDonough and Michael Braungart, while her studio practice relies on materials science and technological collaboration used in tandem with a hands-on craft approach, to imagine appropriate 'product scenarios' for 'multi-life' textiles.

REDESIGN
THE WORLD

Swiss by birth but Italian by adoption, Cornelia Bamert has been passionate about fashion and ethics since her days as a university student in the department of ethnology in Zurich. Now with her own line, Redesign the World, she has been able to combine these passions. After working in the fashion industry for 14 years, with the likes of Antonio Marras, Max&Co and Roberto Cavalli, Bamert embarked on an adventure to combine art and culture to express her taste and ethical sensibilities. As a way of providing development opportunities and enabling cooperation among disadvantaged groups, Bamert blended her personal sense of style with traditional artisanal techniques and crafts. Her philosophy is, 'Make it raw, make it real, but, most importantly, give it a soul!'

Bamert showed her first collection at the Carrousel du Louvre in Paris in 2008. It included pieces produced in Thailand, Mali, Brazil and Italy in collaboration with local artisans. Spurred by her travels and through cooperation with different local fashion houses and artisanal groups, the designer gives young talent the opportunity to gain experience through exchanges and seminars, marrying the concept of socially responsible clothing with the preservation of traditions. Redesign the World's mission is to value and protect imperilled artisanal techniques and traditions and to increase the value of the cultural heritage of different ethnic groups around the world, from the Dogon in Mali to the Karen Hill people in Thailand. Also producing a line of jeans in Italy from recycled fabrics, Bamert gives 12 per cent of revenue to support AIDS research.

This is an ambitious project that integrates and reinterprets tradition, while respecting individual identity. Bamert seeks a different approach to the design and production of women's fashion. Redesign the World is a global patchwork of ancient and modern, folk and vintage, natural fibres and handcrafted pieces.

Producing a single collection each year inspired by a multitude of people and cultures and spurred by chance encounters and creative connections, Bamert collaborates with those she meets on her travels. Using the strengths of each individual or group, she develops her collection in collaboration with local artisans, who become co-creators in the product development.

Warm colours are matched with delicate tones and combined with a melange of varying cultural heritages and reinterpretations of traditional ethnic dress. Compact natural yarns are used for soft oversized cardigans, handcrafted in the heart of the Andes, while fair-trade cotton from Mauritius is used for crisp separates and summer dresses. Glamour is added with crochet produced in the favelas of Rio de Janeiro. Bags are made from fish skin, ponchos from baby alpaca, gloves and shawls from biological wool and jackets and coats from natural latex from the Amazon.

Selling to a select number of boutiques in Italy, Bamert showcases her work at industry trade shows such as the White Show in Milan. She also conducts seminars on ethical design in schools across Italy.

'Make it raw, make it real, but, most importantly, give it a soul!'

Each item in the collection by Redesign the World is inspired and produced by a different ethnic group and tradition in a range of countries, from Mali to Thailand.

Chapter Five

DESIGNER & CORPORATE INITIATIVES

As evidence of the importance of eco-fashion in its myriad forms, many mainstream and avant-garde designers, big and small, have undertaken capsule collections, initiatives or campaigns that involve some form of ethical, ecological or sustainable perspective, finally finding a way to design and produce at least a few pieces in line with their conscience, or alternatively simply reacting to consumer demands and a market hungry for well-designed ethical products. Some of these corporate partnerships have led to some 'uncomfortable bedfellows', as Bono described the RED campaign partners, or controversies, such as, Anya Hindmarch's I'm not a Plastic Bag, produced for Sainsbury's in 2007 as an alternative to using plastic, but which was produced from neither organic nor fair trade cotton in China at low cost, causing accusations of hypocrisy aimed at both the designer and the supermarket. Gap, a major player in the incredible RED campaign, was accused in no uncertain terms by investigative journalist Naomi Klein, in her seminal book *No Logo*, of producing their goods in the now-notorious Free Enterprise Zones in China and around the globe, where tax exemption and marginalized minimum-wage laws keep costs low and where workers rights are equally marginalized.

Nike, now a bastion of ethical and community support, was spurred to this position by its highly publicized use of under-age labour in their overseas production back in the 1990s. USA cut-price giant Walmart, the largest retailer in the world, became the single biggest USA producer of organic cotton in 2009, leading it to state: 'At Wal-Mart, we see sustainability as one of the most important opportunities for both the future of our business and the future of our world.' Previously, however, it had been considered the pariah of the high street, and lambasted in the press for the Kathie Lee Gifford controversy, when child labour was used in the production of her line for Walmart.

According to a quote by Ray Anderson, CEO of Interface Inc, in the book *The Cultural Creatives* by Paul Ray and Sherry Ruth Anderson, 'Business is the largest, wealthiest, most pervasive institution on the Earth...and it's responsible for most of the damage to the environment. We're a major part of the problem, and unless we become part of the solution, it's over.'

The growth of the ethical market is a direct reaction to an industry that has historically abused the environment and its workers' rights. The luxury industry and the high street have come late to these initiatives, but nevertheless are now making up for lost time, at least in some instances: they are now spurring ecology in design to the next level, distancing it from the history of eco-design as boring basics, with some of the best examples of art and fashion that the industry has to offer. Major players, like Walmart and H&M, have the ability to change the minds of a generation when they undertake sustainability and fair trade as part of their mission. At the same time, luxury designers, the most influential group of design professionals in the fashion industry, make ecology inspirational. Vivienne Westwood's heartfelt pleas to reduce carbon emissions through her DIY collection and Yves Saint Laurent's upcycling of pre-consumer waste are examples of what will drive ecology in design into the future.

Phillipe Stark, best known for designing interiors and products, brought his sense of scale and propotion to this mens- and womenswear collection, produced by Scottish knitwear company, Ballantyne.

AGATHA RUIZ DE LA PRADA

Born in Madrid, Spain, Agatha Ruiz de la Prada y Sentmenat is perhaps one of Spain's best-known personalities in the fashion industry. Known for her riotous use of dazzling colours and large graphic prints, she is most famous for her use of such motifs as giant hearts, egg-yolk-centred daisies, stars and enormous pouting lips. Her clothes, often accessorized with these giant motifs, are alternately sculptural, dimensional, void of extraneous embellishment, simple and clean in line, but oversized and fluid in brilliant coloured knits. Her work is often reminiscent of a candy-coloured piñata explosion, Dalí- or Picasso-esque in its combination of depth and childlike simplicity. Outrageous, playful and conceptual – you cannot help but smile looking at her designs.

Her vibrant colours and graphics adorn a dizzying array of products, including kitchenware, bed linen, fragrances, ceramics, children's toys, furniture, spectacles, motorcycle helmets, computer games, pet accessories and MP3 players. Ruiz de la Prada also manages multiple licensing agreements for such items as household paint, mattresses and a child's playground, each item instantly recognizable by its use of colour and print. She has also collaborated on a collection of dress watches for Swatch, a line of costume jewellery for El Corte Inglés and a mobile phone for Vodafone.

As an artist, she has participated in many exhibitions and shows, including expositions of her drawings and hand-painted outfits in Madrid art galleries, a show of 'Agathized' kimonos in Osaka, Japan, the 'Absolut Ruiz de la Prada' roadshow, an exhibition entitled 'A tribute to Chillida' at the Museo Reina Sofía in Madrid, exhibitions of her work at the Museum of Modern Art in Paris during fashion week and a presentation of a wedding dress made entirely from porcelain at the IVAM in Valencia. She is the recipient of multiple awards, including the Fashion Oscar in Italy for best foreign designer in 2004, the Colombia es Pasion award for her support of young Colombian designers, the Prix de la Moda from *Marie Claire* magazine, the Top Glamour Award from *Glamour* magazine for the best designer of the year and the New Yorker Award from the US Chamber of Commerce in Spain, all in 2007. →

Famous for her iconic use of moons, stars, suns and hearts, as well as her use of brilliant colours, Agatha Ruiz de la Prada creates surrealistic clothing designs, including a charity Xmas Tree Dress for yoox.com.

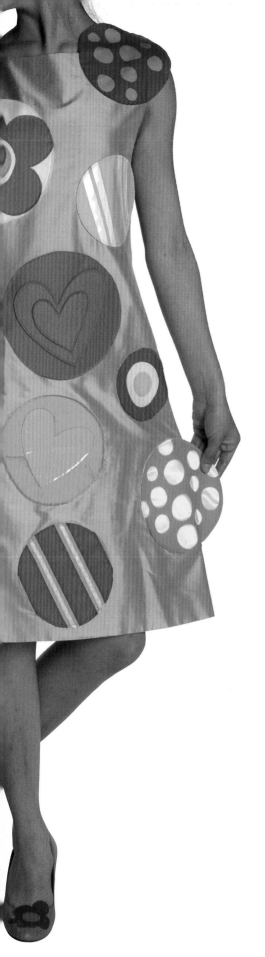

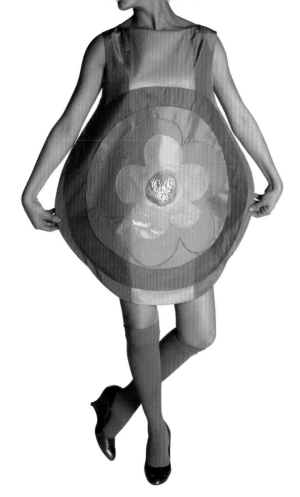

Her background is one of intellectualism and art appreciation, being one of the leading figures in the sociocultural movement of the 1980s known as 'La Movida Madrileña' ('The Madrilenian Groove'). She continues to participate in multiple cultural events, including the Thursday Gatherings of intellectuals and artists at her Madrid studio. She has presented her collections on the catwalks of Madrid, Barcelona, Milan, Florence, Paris, Puerto Rico, Zagreb, Warsaw, Columbia, Santo Domingo, Athens and Sarajevo. Her distribution includes the USA, South America, Korea and Russia.

Known for her support of Spain's green party, The Confederation of the Greens, Ruiz de la Prada was one of 16 top fashion designers invited by Greenpeace to participate in a Madrid fashion show entitled 'Moda sin Tóxicos' ('Fashion Without Toxics') in 2006. Exclusive creations were designed to draw attention to the use of toxic chemicals, currently widely used in clothing and textile manufacture, and the serious immune and nervous-system diseases caused by exposure to chemicals, specifically reproductive disorders and cancer. The designers joined together to lobby for the phasing out of chemicals and their replacement with safer alternatives. Ruiz de la Prada created an Xmas Tree Dress, available exclusively for yoox.com, the proceeds from which were donated to Greenpeace. The piece, in classic Ruiz de la Prada style, was in brilliant lime-coloured wool adorned with scarlet hearts and featuring side fins to mimic the shape of a Christmas tree. Ruiz de la Prada has also collaborated with UNICEF.

BARNEYS NEW YORK

A mecca for discerning fashionistas and clothing connoisseurs, Barneys New York was founded in 1923 by Barney Pressman, who raised the US$500 necessary to lease the premises by pawning his wife's engagement ring. The store initially sold discounted men's tailored clothing. It was not until 1964 that Barneys shed its discount image, moving upmarket by introducing European designer collections and becoming the first USA retailer to stock the entire Giorgio Armani menswear collection. The store carried a range of mechandise from denim to high-end men's suits and also sold Hubert de Givenchy, Christian Dior and Pierre Cardin. Women's clothing was not introduced until 1976, along with housewares, cosmetics and a restaurant.

Now a chain of luxury department stores comprising several large stores in New York City, Beverly Hills, Chicago, Las Vegas and Boston, and multiple smaller stores in various other locations across the USA, Barneys focuses on luxury women's designer apparel. The store is famous for its merhcandising mix, offering a younger, casual range of designers and labels in a more relaxed environment than many of their high-end competitors. Barneys is a Manhattan institution, an emporium of style and a celebrity hang-out. It has been featured in a number of hip television series such as *Friends*, *Sex in the City* and *Seinfeld*.

Under the auspices of senior vice president and fashion director Julie Gilhart, Barneys has become known as *the* high-end eco-conscious store, signing multiple exclusive deals for ecological and sustainable merchandise and undertaking various promotions, such as the green Christmas campaign in 2007, during which store windows, advertising, bags, gift cards and catalogues all displayed the environmental theme. The now-famous windows, created by Simon Doonan, presented Rudolph the Recycling Reindeer, the Twelve Green Days of Christmas, and the Heroes of Green. A percentage of sales benefited environmental charities such as 'The Climate Project' and amFAR, while Barneys also made a commitment to plant 25,000 trees to help offset its carbon footprint. The company stated: 'We thought it was time to add a little charm and levity to this important issue.'

In 2007, Barneys made a major commitment to promote and feature organic and sustainable products in its stores with the introduction of the Loomstate collection designed by Rogan Gregory, the same designer behind eco-lines Rogan and the iconic Edun. Other featured eco-collections have included Koi Suwannagate's organic silk →

With multiple exclusive design collaborations, including Theory, Philip Lim, Loomstate and YSL, Barneys have become synonymous with green design.

'The Green movement has produced a surge of creativity in the design community. We are anxious to introduce our customers to this new wave of sustainable luxury.'

and vintage cashmere collection, Raf Simons for Jil Sander's organic knits made from 100 per cent organic cashmere and Yves Saint Laurent's 'New Vintage' collection, made from upcycled YSL pre-consumer textile waste. According to Julie Gilhart, 'We're going to keep offering new things and trying to find new people who are conscious of the way they're doing things…. We're celebrating craftsmanship and limited product.'

In collaboration with Loomstate, Barneys offered a limited initiative where consumers could bring in their old T-shirts and have them refashioned with cool graphics by Loomstate, while donating one per cent of sales to 'The Climate Project'. Scott Hahn, co-founder of Loomstate, which uses 100 per cent organic cotton in the manufacture of its products, believes that what comes from the soil should go back to the soil, turning waste into fashion with the T-shirt project. Barneys also held an event encouraging customers to recycle their worn jeans by exchanging them in return for a discount on new jeans. According to Howard Socol, former CEO of Barneys, 'The Green movement has produced a surge of creativity in the design community. We are anxious to introduce our customers to this new wave of sustainable luxury.'

Barneys, Barneys CO-OP and Barneys outlets are located across the USA and products are also available online.

H&M & DESIGNERS AGAINST AIDS

Swedish giant Hennes & Mauritz, innovator of designer collaborations for hundreds of its stores in more than 30 countries, produces a product range that encompasses make-up, accessories and ready-to-wear fashion. The company's ethos of providing fashion at unbeatable prices has doubled its turnover in the last five years. Specializing in hot-off-the-catwalk looks, the retailer not only appeals to the junior market but also to all ages and income brackets, with basics as trend-forward items. Offering designer diffusion lines and mini-collections with major name partners, such as Karl Lagerfeld, Comme des Garçons, Roberto Cavalli and Stella McCartney, this high-street retailer created an instant demand for its products. Pioneering the 'just-in-time' retail concept alongside Spanish brand Zara, H&M updates store offerings daily.

With corporate social responsibility initiatives in cooperation with UNICEF, H&M is a member of the Better Cotton Initiative that seeks the improvement of growing conditions of conventional cotton. The company also signed the 'Seal the Deal' agreement in advance of the UN's Climate Change Conference in Copenhagen in 2009, calling for a climate agreement that is fair, balanced and effective. Furthermore, H&M has endorsed the Water Mandate, a voluntary initiative set up by the United Nations Global Compact, committing partners to address water sustainability issues.

Initiated in Belgium in 2005, the Designers Against AIDS (DAA) project provides a vehicle to raise awareness about HIV/AIDS with young people all over the world. High-profile celebrities from the worlds of music, fashion, sports and art design prints and graphics that are transposed onto T-shirts, hoodies, underwear and nightwear for men and women, and sold through H&M stores worldwide. Presenting different items each season, the DAA collection is promoted through its website, as well as through fashion, concept and music stores. Belgian company sense-organics (see page 42) supply the T-shirt blanks on a not-for-profit basis, while all the artists donate their time and creativity for free. All items are fair trade produced and made from pesticide-free cotton. Kirsten Weihe-Keidel from the company explains how, 'it doesn't make much sense to try and keep people healthy but, at the same time kill the planet they live on.'

The main focus for DAA is the website, www.designersagainstaids.com, where each design and designer is showcased with links to local AIDS organizations, along with press releases, publications and quotes from the celebrities. The DAA website is available in English, French, Spanish, German, Italian, Dutch, Russian, Chinese, Finnish and Japanese, with an Arabic translation in the works. →

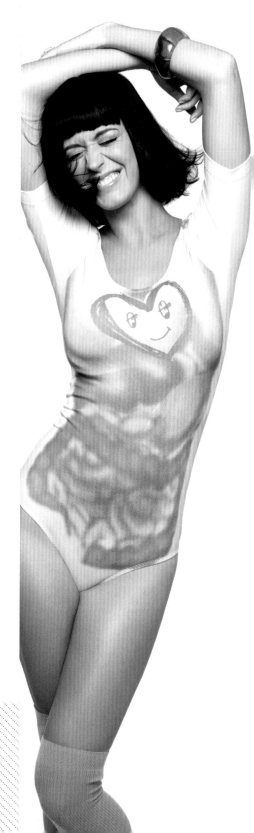

The DAA collection through H&M promotes
AIDS awareness through the use of celebrity
designers, and donates 25 per cent of profits to
AIDS awareness programmes.

In 2008, DAA presented a collection of T-shirts and hooded sweaters designed by Francisco Costa for Calvin Klein, Playboy Design, Robert Smith from The Cure, Rogan Gregory, Chicks on Speed and Mingface, to mention just a few. In the same year they also launched a collection of T-shirts, tank tops and hooded sweaters through H&M under the 'Fashion Against AIDS' label, and designed by the world's most acclaimed musicians and fashion designers, such as Timberland, Good Charlotte, Jade Jagger, Ziggy Marley, Katharine Hamnett and Rihanna. The collection was sold and promoted in H&M stores across 27 countries. The artists participated free of charge and all net proceeds from sales, calculated as 25 per cent of the sales price, went to AIDS-awareness programmes coordinated by DAA. This unique arrangement was accepted by H&M in light of both the artists and sense-organics donating their time and talent for free, with H&M to its credit agreeing.

There is now a second 'Fashion against AIDS' collection at H&M, sold in over 900 stores in 30 countries, and produced in conjunction with Dita Von Tesse, Cyndi Lauper and Tokio Hotel. DAA is also working with Katharine Hamnett on a reusable organic-cotton shopping bag, which they intend to supply to all major fashion chains and supermarkets in a variety of colours, offering a trendy and stylish alternative to plastic bags, and with part of the proceeds going to both eco- and HIV/AIDS-awareness projects.

DAA has featured on MTV and Fashion TV and articles have appeared in many magazines and newspapers around the world, including *i-D*, *Vogue*, *Elle*, *Marie Claire*, *Vanity Fair*, *Cosmopolitan*, *The International Herald Tribune*, *El Mundo*, *Libération*, *New York Post* and *Le Monde*.

Arty, playful, edgy and tongue-in-cheek graphics are used to adorn the collection of T-shirts, hoodies, body suits and lingerie produced by DAA for H&M.

KATHARINE HAMNETT

Katharine Hamnett was launched into fame in the 1980s. Selling to successful high-end retailers, her sales boomed worldwide. Honoured with the Cotton Designer of the Year Award in 1983, she pioneered the techniques of garment dyeing, stonewashing and distressing denim. The same year saw the launch of her slogan T-shirt, '58% don't want Pershing', which she so famously wore to a meeting with then prime minister Margaret Thatcher at Downing Street. The T-shirt protested against the proliferation of Pershing and cruise nuclear missiles. At a time of political discontent in the UK, Hamnett became the voice of a generation who felt powerless to effect positive change. The T-shirts were sported by high-profile celebrities of the day, including The Beatles, Princess Diana, Madonna and George Michael.

Ongoing research into the fashion industry's abuses motivated Hamnett to change the way she did business. Horrified by the discovery that millions of people in the garment industry were working under intolerable conditions, she attempted to effect change from within by campaigning for the industry, including her own licensees, to produce ethically and sustainably. By mid-2000, however, she changed her focus to raising consumer awareness of the clothing industry's abuses: 'I discovered the fashion industry was responsible for a living environmental nightmare.'

Visiting Mali at the invitation of Oxfam in 2003, she saw first-hand the human suffering caused by conventional cotton farming. In 2004, she relaunched the Katharine E. Hamnett mens- and womenswear slogan T-shirt line, made from organic cotton and to the highest ethical and environmental standards. Many of the original slogans were just as relevant in a world torn apart by war, economic depression and conflict as they were back in the 1980s. Slogans include 'Choose Life', inspired by the Buddhist concept of making a living without hurting anyone or anything; 'Clean Up or Die', a comment on the future of humankind if existing polluting and wasteful practices are not eliminated; 'Education not Missiles', a plea to invest in the true source of a nation's wealth; 'Use a Condom', a reference to the continued worldwide rise in cases of HIV; 'Make Trouble', a request to question everything; 'Save the Rainforests', an urgent appeal to stop clearcutting; 'No War', a statement that war is the worst form of environmental disaster; and 'Stop and Think', posing the question what would happen if instead of bombing →

All Katharine Hamnett logo T-shirts are made from organic cotton to the highest ethical and environmental standards.

'I discovered the fashion industry was responsible for a living environmental nightmare'.

the country that Osama bin Laden was in, we had asked why these people hate us so much. Hamnett explains, 'Just because it is convention or the law doesn't mean it is right. Nor does it mean it can't be changed.'

The Free Burma Campaign T-shirts, launched in collaboration with Prospect Burma, draw attention to a country suffering under a brutal military dictatorship that refuses to transfer power to the legally elected government of the country, led by Nobel Peace laureate Daw Aung San Suu Kyi. The charity, endorsed by Suu Kyi, believes that the best means of bringing positive change to Burma is to invest in the education of its young people. With many universities closed by the ruling military government, a whole generation has been deprived of an education. Prospect Burma's mission is to invest in the democratic future of Burma through the education of Burmese students through scholarships. Students, many of whom are refugees, study subjects vital to the redevelopment of Burma, including public health, education and economics. From the sale of each T-shirt, £15 (US$22) is donated directly to the registered educational charity Prospect Burma.

Issues raised by Hamnett's iconic T-shirts have inspired a whole new generation of conscience-aware celebrities to sport the messages publicly, including Peaches Geldof and the band Dirty Pretty Things. The T-shirts are available online.

The Katharine Hamnett logo T-shirt collection has been celebrating activism and freedom of speech since the 1980s.

MIGUEL ADROVER

Self-taught Spanish-born designer Miguel Adrover captured the fashion industry's imagination with three consecutive collections between 2000 and 2002, for which he received the prestigious Perry Ellis Award and the VH1 Fashion Award. Upstaging major name designers during New York's Fashion Week, Adrover showed his collections in such alternative venues as a Lower East Side theatre, a synagogue, an East Village park and a school courtyard. Taking the industry by storm, Adrover has featured in a diverse range of magazines from *Vogue* to *Paper*, which praised his talent, wit and craftsmanship. Packing top-level editors such as Anna Wintour into these unlikely locations, Adrover also had buyers line up to place orders, with some retailers even offering to finance production in order to get their orders fulfilled.

Innovative and inventive, Adrover undertook an anti-label reconstruction of brands like Louis Vuitton, Burberry and Ralph Lauren, creating miniskirts and strapless dresses to die for and causing an industry-wide sensation. His show themes were an exercise in social commentary, drawing attention to the plight of the New York homeless and the American way of life. His slim tailoring, bias cuts, intricate beading and fabric treatments showcased his talent and his understanding of fabric. His designs, often cerebral and sculptural, were always superbly executed. Often criticized for his political statements, Adrover views fashion as a medium for social message. 'If it is possible to create a political or social awareness in connection with attractive apparel, then that is a goal for me. My collections attempt to open up the eyes of the people for our society.'

Plagued by sourcing, production, pricing and shipping issues, Adrover's career suffered several catastrophic stops and starts. After signing with the now defunct Pegasus Group (who closed its doors in 2001), he has since been actively involved in exploring the relationship between fashion and the arts, through his participation in exhibitions at the Bellevue Arts Museum in Washington, the Museo Reina Sofía in Madrid, the Victoria & Albert Museum in London and the Metropolitan Museum of Art in New York.

Now creative director of eco-friendly clothing company hessnatur, Adrover has found a new home. Founded 30 years ago by the European environmentalist Heinz Hess, the company designs organic and natural clothing. Priding itself on the authenticity of its heritage, compassion and respect towards the planet and its people, hessnatur employs natural processes to create its clothing. The company states, 'Respect for the planet and its people is fundamental to the way we do business, interact with our customers, our partners and each other. We will not compromise our environmental integrity or our design aesthetics.' →

One hundred per cent alpaca, organic silk, cashmere and pure merino wool form the basis of the Miguel Adrover collection for hessnatur.

'For me, it is something so powerful. By working in mainstream, I can help people realize the clothes they wear affect the environment.'

With a goal of being 100 per cent organic in everything it makes, hessnatur uses only pure organic cotton and other luxurious natural fibres, such as silk, alpaca, cashmere and wool. Overall, organic fabric use is limited to between 22 and 55 per cent of the collection, but all textiles used are pure and natural. Clothing is made by people whose human rights are respected, and hessnatur has set the standard for humane working conditions, working alongside the Clean Clothes Campaign. In partnership with renowned Nobel Peace prizewinner Muhammad Yunus and the Grameen Foundation, hessnatur works with Grameen's non-profit subsidiary, Grameen Knitwear in Dhaka, Bangladesh. Adrover also designed a limited-edition organic-cotton T-shirt exclusively for Whole Foods, with the message 'The World is in your Hands', with 15 per cent of all sales going to the hessnatur scholarship fund at the Grameen Shikkha Project in Bangladesh. The line is available online through the hessnatur website.

Environmental integrity and design aesthetics are the bedrock of Adrover's work for hessnatur, incorporating nature-inspired jacquards and knits made with fair trade principles in Peru.

PHILIPPE STARCK

Known worldwide for his trendy restaurants and award-winning hotels, Philippe Starck is equally renowned and respected for his product and interior designs. As one of the best-known designers from the Milanese school of New Design, Starck considers the democratization of design his duty, unlike his counterparts who produce provocative, expensive, single items. Designing products to reach the maximum number of people, Starck worked with USA retail giant Target to create a range of everyday products for the home, office, kitchen and bathroom, infusing practical objects with charm, playfulness and invention. The designer's long-held belief in elevating the joy that can be found in simple things necessitated the synergistic relationship he is famous for, that of combining common, cheap materials with high design. Iconic designs have included the Juicy Salif, a juicer he created for Italian company Alessi, an optical mouse for Microsoft and the transparent Louis Ghost chair.

With an impressive list of collaborations, Starck has worked in partnership with Alain Mikli to create Starck Eyes for Mikli since 1996, reinventing the category of ergonomic glasses, and with Fossil in recent years to develop elegant and intelligent watches. Starck Naked for Puma since 2004 saw the designer continue his history of successful collaborations by creating 'intelligent shoes' and technical and elegantly sexy underclothes for men and women. He has been described as 'a crazy genius, revolutionary, subversive, a visionary'.

Starck's first foray into a fashion collection of men's and women's coordinates was in partnership with the historic Scottish knitwear house Ballantyne. Founded in 1921, the house is famous for its intricate cashmere intarsia designs. The materials and garments for the collection were developed and researched at the Ballantyne workshop in Innerleithen, Scotland, to represent exactly the timeless vision of Philippe Starck. The collection comprises 30 pieces for men and 30 pieces for women. It is a combination of multifunctional garments with ergonomic designs and contemporary fittings, in line with the needs of modern life. These seriously designed pieces nevertheless incorporate Starck's signature of design humour. Using waterproof →

'The public will take maybe three years to understand the concept. It's not fashion. But intelligent people will know to discover us.'

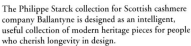

The Philippe Starck collection for Scottish cashmere company Ballantyne is designed as an intelligent, useful collection of modern heritage pieces for people who cherish longevity in design.

cashmere knits with technical fabrics and silk linings, Starck creates lightweight multifunctioning pieces, featuring detachable waistcoats, double-position collars, fluorescent contrasting linings and pockets deliberately camouflaged to maintain the purity of the silhouette. The simple, clean, Zen-like designs are intended as a range of wearable, functional and interchangeable basics. Taking such a marked departure from the fashion system, Starck considers, 'The public will take maybe three years to understand the concept. It's not fashion. But intelligent people will know to discover us.'

The collection is aimed at people who cherish longevity and who appreciate elegance, intelligent design and innovation. Starck believes that his made-in-Scotland 'intelligent cashmere' line will defy trendiness and be the antithesis of fashion, which he sees as a fickle industry that is marked by such a high turnover that it gives birth to 'a system of consumption and over-consumption that has no future'. The collection comprises a complete wardrobe, including knit dresses, hooded cardigans, jackets and car coats, all with a natural elegance. Starck's vision was to emphasize the natural versatility of cashmere in a modern but timeless way, to express sexiness and desirability: 'I decided to collaborate with Ballantyne because of their ancestral know-how, their strong expertise in cashmere and the Scottish roots of the company.'

The collection is available in Ballantyne stores across the globe and inevitably has garnered worldwide press coverage in *Vogue*, *The Guardian*, *Harper's Bazaar*, *Drapers*, *Esquire*, *WWD*, *Collezioni* and *Wallpaper*.

SALVATORE FERRAGAMO

With over 500 stores, Ferragamo is one of the world's leading luxury-goods manufacturers, producing shoes, leather goods, ready-to-wear, silk products, accessories and fragrances. Born in 1898, Salvatore Ferragamo came from very humble beginnings in Bonita, Southern Italy, making his first pair of shoes at the age of nine for his sister's confirmation. One of 14 children, Salvatore emigrated in 1914 to the USA. In 1923, he founded the Hollywood Boot Shop in Hollywood, California, producing high-end, custom-made shoes by hand for silent-movie stars such as Clara Bow and Mary Pickford, becoming known as shoemaker to the stars at the formation of the burgeoning Californian film industry. Moving back to Italy in 1927, this time to Florence, he made fashion shoes for some of the wealthiest and most famous women of the century, including the Maharani of Cooch Behar, Eva Perón, Greta Garbo, Sophia Loren and Marilyn Monroe. He invented new techniques, pioneered the use of new materials and made an entirely new shoe last, taking great pride in making well-fitting, comfortable, handmade shoes. Renowned for conceiving the wedge shoe, he also introduced the invisible shoe and the cage heel. Ferragamo worked through bankruptcy, the German occupation of Italy and Mussolini to become one of the world's most successful luxury-shoe manufacturers.

The company has been creating ecological handbags since 2007, when it introduced the Alice Leather bag. Since that time, it has produced a collection of bags made only from natural, chemical-free and non-polluting materials. The focus on eco-fabrics has expanded from a single style in 2007 to two separate collections in a matter of only a few short years. The main component of the eco-bag collection is the natural, metal-free leather that is treated with natural essences and coloured with chemical-free products. Other components used in the manufacture of the bag, such as the lining, padding and closures, are also non-polluting and made exclusively for the brand. Linings, for example, are made entirely from natural hemp and produced without the use of pesticides. The colours are natural, ocean blue and caramel. →

The Ferragamo Eco Collection consists of a series of vegetable-tanned leather bags that exclude any metal hardware, and feature linings made of natural hemp.

Although leather is a natural material, the finishing of the skins is generally a toxic process, with the use of metals and other contaminants, not to mention the pollution of large quantities of water. Metal-free tanning is a process developed and certified in 2001 by a group of chemical experts. It makes the leather biodegradable and renders the skins water resistant, while maintaining the suppleness and softness of the skins by using vegetable oil extracted through the pressing of special seeds and plants. The process of certifying the leather metal-free is not dissimilar to that of certifying organic cotton. All production must be kept entirely separate from general production so there is no possibility of contaminating the skins, much like organic cotton must be processed entirely separately from conventional cotton. The tanning method requires a kind of pickling procedure, with skins tumbled in barrels along with tannins from tree bark, similar to those used in the wine industry. As with most certified organic processes, the production is strictly monitored by external bodies.

The collection of metal-free leather bags consists of three special and iconic styles separate from the greater whole of the Ferragamo bag collection. None of the bags use any metal hardware, with all closures made entirely of leather, including worked-leather slides, tabs, clasps, rings and ties. Each style is enriched with stitching details, contrast bindings and the distinctive Ferragamo workmanship. Designs are softly and elegantly tucked and pleated into subtle bow shapes, gathered in with fine leather ties and softly styled into bulbous and slouchy shapes, rounded out with a modern functional style.

The Salvatore Ferragamo Eco Collection is sold through Ferragamo's own stand-alone stores, as well as in high-end department stores worldwide.

VIVIENNE WESTWOOD

Few designers in recent history have been more influential than Dame Vivienne Westwood. Always the activist, she first came to the attention of the press and public when outfitting the seminal UK punk band The Sex Pistols for their first live gig. Westwood and partner Malcolm McLaren, then manager of The Sex Pistols, were influenced by the Situationists, a group of international Marxist-style revolutionaries who favoured human primitive desires and the pursuance of passion over capitalism. Egalitarian and anti-establishment from the start, Westwood opened the store Seditionaries on the King's Road, London, which became emblematic of the groundbreaking punk scene in the UK, and where she sold her outrageous designs incorporating bondage, safety pins, razor blades, chains and dog collars. She is single-handedly responsible for the introduction of the dog collar as jewellery and the subversion of Scottish plaids to the punk aesthetic. The store, still owned by Westwood to this day, is now known as World's End, where her Anglomania collection retails.

Widely known as a political activist, Westwood has attended and campaigned for nuclear disarmament. She also joined forces with the British civil-rights group Liberty. Westwood launched an exclusive limited-edition T-shirt emblazoned with the slogan 'I am not a terrorist, please don't arrest me', in an effort to defend habeas corpus, a statement for civil liberty and democracy. All funds from the sale went towards the campaign.

Westwood is famous for sending down the runway at least one political slogan T-shirt a season; her 2009 statement was: 'We need an estimated $30 billion per year to save the rainforest'. This inspired the collection's 'Do It Yourself' conservation theme, alternatively dubbed 'bed-sheet couture'. Draped, wrapped and cowled fabric lengths were fashioned into demure sarong-style day dresses and paired with men's knee-length football socks and precariously high platform shoes. Single 3-metre lengths of double-faced duchess satin and rich brocade, intact of selvedges, were belted, tied and draped around the body to form wraps and capes and teamed with low-slung open-seamed trousers, revealing men's boxer shorts underneath. The implicit statement was one of democratization and empowerment, with the intent to inspire anyone to create their own couture from a beautiful tablecloth or curtain, while borrowing their boyfriend's undies and socks to complete the look. In an interview with Jonathan Ross in 2009, the designer said, 'Don't spend money, just take what you can find, take your old things, keep on wearing them. Don't buy much fashion anymore but if you do buy it, choose really well, wear it for a long time.' →

Assymetric drapes in silk and bold striped knits are combined with silk charmeuse and wrapped into sari and sarong styles by Vivienne Westwood.

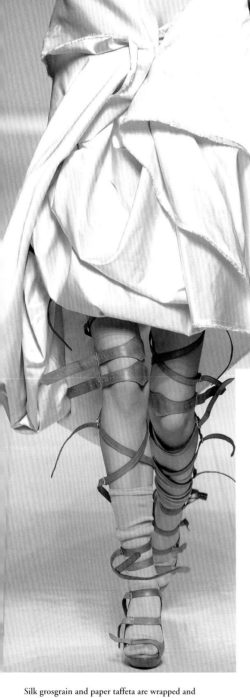

Silk grosgrain and paper taffeta are wrapped and tied into cocooning drapes and paired with men's pleated shorts for the Do It Yourself collection by Vivienne Westwood.

On Ross's popular evening television talk show, Westwood appealed to the public to reduce their carbon dioxide emissions by making individual lifestyle changes, in an attempt to sway public opinion. Explaining that global warming is one item of many on most politicians' long to-do lists, she urged the public to take independent positive action. Citing global warming as the root of many other issues, including the economic crisis, Westwood went on to talk in great detail about climate crises and the disastrous effects of a simple rise of three degrees in temperature. In a heartfelt plea, she listed a litany of global disasters that would result in devastating temperature rise, sparking famine, migration and war, with the toll of human suffering as a price just too steep to pay. A three-degree rise in temperature will bring about a chain reaction that dominoes and accelerates until runaway global warming is achieved and cannot then be stopped, resulting in the destruction of the rainforest, and ultimately humankind. Westwood concluded, 'The public needs to know all this. If you are going to reverse it, the speed with which you do it is the most important thing. We need government policy and we need these issues really talked about. You have got to get involved if the human race is going to survive.'

YEOHLEE TENG

Moving to New York from Malaysia, Yeohlee Teng established her own design house, Yeohlee Incorporated, in 1981. She is known and respected in the industry as the 'designer's designer', and her work is intelligent, cerebral, architectural and iconically New Yorkian. She is perhaps one of the USA's best-kept design secrets. The late Richard Martin, chief curator of the Metropolitan Museum of Art, called her, 'one of the most ingenious makers of clothing today'.

As an artist who uses fabric and the human body to express her three-dimensional concepts, she has exhibited her work widely and is in many ways more akin to a fine artist than a designer. A 1998 exhibition in the Aedes East Gallery in Berlin paralleled her clothing designs with the work of architect Ken Yeang. Showing her work in 2000 at the Galleria Museum in Paris, alongside Hussein Chalayan, Rei Kawakubo, Alexander McQueen, Issey Miyake and Yves Saint Laurent, the exhibition explored how fibres and fabrics have driven twentieth-century clothing design. The Victoria & Albert Museum in London showcased her work in 'Fashion in Motion', with her work now on permanent display in the museum's dress gallery. The Fashion Institute of Technology's museum curator, Dr Valerie Steele, displayed Yeohlee's work in an exhibition on the relationship between clothing and the body, the individual and the environment, explaining why Yeohlee's work has been described as 'intimate architecture'.

In 2005, Yeohlee's work was showcased at the Kennedy Center for the Performing Arts' 'New China Chic' exhibition, which brought together work from a diverse range of international designers of Chinese ancestry, and was also shown at the Corcoran Gallery of Art. Her work has featured in 'The Fashion of Architecture' at the AIA Center for Architecture in New York, in 'Love and War' at the Fashion Institute of Technology and in 'Skin and Bones' at The Museum of Contemporary Art in Los Angeles. These shows again paralleled her designs with architecture and placed her work alongside fashion luminaries Alexander McQueen, Viktor & Rolf, Dries Van Noten, Alber Elbaz, Junya Watanabe and architects Herzog & de Meuron, Rem Koolhaas, Frank Gehry, Jean Nouvel and Kazuyo Sejima.

Nominated with Marc Jacobs and Narciso Rodriguez for the 2004 Fashion Design Award by the Smithsonian Cooper-Hewitt, National Design Museum, she was awarded the prize for her contribution to American fashion excellence. Yeohlee believes that 'clothes have magic', and that her clothing works on a practical as well as a psychological level. She designs year-round, seasonless clothes for the 'urban nomad', a term she coined for her autumn 1997 collection. Believing that design serves a function, which is refined through time and process, she is driven and defined by her use of material, creating poetry through the process of design. →

Created from utilitarian fabrics, Yeohlee Teng's collection draws on the principle of economy in design, with modular and functional pieces.

Drawing on the principle of economy in design, fabric and execution, Yeohlee created her autumn 2009 collection with zero waste, using every single inch of fabric, with not a scrap of material wasted. She created modular, functional and versatile designs crafted from utilitarian fabrics, each piece made from triangles, squares, rectangles or combinations thereof. This pared-down bare-bones collection exhibited her signature minimal Zen aesthetic and a sense of primal efficiency. The mood of the collection resonated with Edward Burtynsky's photographs of quarries and urban mines. The inverted cubed architecture of his quarries echoes Yeohlee's signature geometrics. Strangely urban pinstriped sarongs cascade in mimicry of the dark scarred landscape of urban mines. Utilitarian black denim is cut into architectural swing jackets and quarry coats with angular cropped sleeves and dimensional roll collars. Black rubberized felt is reminiscent of the slick oily ground in Burtynsky's photographs of industrial waste, while molten-metal jersey pours over the body to envelop the figure in dripping triangles, rectangles and squares. Fabrics include double-faced angora and wool, alpaca and carbon-felted silk, while colours range from coal black through jet and anthracite to liquid silver.

The shape and mood of Yeohlee's zero-waste collection was inspired by the industrial landscape photographs of Edward Burtynsky.

Yeohlee has featured in a range of industry papers, such as *WWD*, and in alternative magazines like *Soma*, *Paper* and *Surface*, as well as in newspapers such as *The International Herald Tribune*, *The Los Angeles Times*, *The Financial Times* and online journals. Current and past collections can be viewed at Yeohlee's website, and the collection is available at high-end retailers, department stores and museum shops around the world.

YVES SAINT LAURENT

Yves Saint Laurent is one of the pre-eminent couture fashion houses in the world, its name ubiquitous with couture and luxury design. One of the world's leading labels for fashion, perfumes, accessories, make-up, skincare and haute couture, Yves Saint Laurent currently has more than 60 independent stores, including flagship stores in Paris, New York, London, Milan, Hong Kong and Tokyo, as well as selling in the most prestigious multibrand boutiques and department stores around the world.

Born in French Algeria, Yves Mathieu Saint Laurent moved to Paris and joined the house of Christian Dior at the age of 19, assuming creative direction of the house in 1957 at the tender age of 21, after the death of Christian Dior. After returning to Paris following a term of National Service, Saint Laurent founded his own house in 1962 with friend and partner Pierre Bergé. Famous for popularizing the 'ethnic' look with his 'Out of Africa' collection, which included the safari-jacket pantsuit, he most importantly conceived the iconic tuxedo suit and smoking jacket for women, which quickly became mainstays of the collections. He is also renowned for his beaded and jewelled pieces inspired by Picasso paintings and the 1965 Mondrian collection.

The designer has received countless commendations and accolades, including the prestigious Neiman Marcus Award in 1958 and the Council of Fashion Designers of America's International Fashion Award in 1981. He was made a Chevalier of the Legion of Honour, then promoted to the rank of Officer and finally to Commandeur in 2001. A national icon, Yves Saint Laurent marked the fortieth anniversary of his work with a retrospective at the final of the 1998 World Cup in front of 80,000 football fans and on more than 170 international sports channels. The Metropolitan Museum of Art in New York mounted a 25-year retrospective of his work in 1983, directed by Diana Vreeland, the largest retrospective ever granted to a living designer.

The company was sold first to a French pharmaceutical giant and then to the Gucci Group, during which time the collections have been designed by Alber Elbaz and Tom Ford. The couture house closed in 2002, when Yves Saint Laurent retired after being dogged by years of poor health, drug abuse and depression. The brand nevertheless carries on the legacy, with a prêt-à-porter collection produced under the creative direction of Stefano Pilati.

The company's first foray into the world of ecological production was the upcycling and recycling of vintage YSL fabric remnants into a capsule collection of exclusive items that were unveiled at Barneys New York in June 2009. The YSL 'New Vintage' collection, designed by Stefano Pilati, is the brand's definitive commentary on the unforgiving speed of fashion trends, while simultaneously satisfying the demands of the luxury ethical shopper. Pilati explains, 'For me, my aim was…to give fashion a value that is a bit beyond the visual aspect or the consuming aspect.'

The collection is made exclusively from recycled cotton drill from overages from the Tom Ford era of the YSL archives. Choosing not to go down the more obvious route of incorporating →

Reusing vintage remnants from an earlier era of Yves Saint Laurent's work, Stefano Pilati, creative director of the company, refashions them into the 'New Vintage' collection.

organic fabric into the collection, Pilati instead decided to use the company's own pre-consumer waste rather than purchase and consume more fabric. Pilati credits Barneys fashion director Julie Gilhart with encouraging him to produce the collection, which incorporates more than 60 pieces and includes handbags and shoes at the luxury price point. Each item features a special 'New Vintage' label and sports a limited-edition number, underscoring the limited nature of the collection. By halfway through the Barneys launch party most of the pieces had been sold. Articulating YSL's aim for a collection 'manifesto', Pilati called the 'New Vintage' collection 'a general attempt to give a sensibility and an education to our public so that it can act consciously toward its environment…using known codes and a common language that are reassuring and familiar.' Pilati was looking to redirect focus on the traditions, skills and know-how of the house, rather than the desire to consume, which compromises and distorts the system of evaluation and integrity. He concludes, 'New Vintage is my way to reflect our social and economic state by capitalizing on existing resources to translate sustainable "values" into "forms".'

Glossary

abaya: A full-length, sleeveless outer garment worn by Arabs.

Action Aid: A UK charity that tackles the effects of poverty.

AIAB: An Italian association for the certification of organic fibre and fabric.

Aid to Artisans: A US organization that helps artisans to develop their products locally and market them worldwide.

Azo: Compounds that produce vivid colours in the dyeing process, some forms of which have been found to be carcinogenic.

bamboo fabric: A woven or knitted fabric made from the soft fibrous pulp of the bamboo plant.

basting stitch: A running stitch that is generally used to keep a piece of fabric in place temporarily.

Best Management Practices (BMP): An Australian body for the certification of cotton fibre as it pertains to environmental and ethical stewardship.

Better Cotton Initiative: An international organization that aims to promote measurable improvements in the key environmental and social impacts of cotton cultivation worldwide to make it more economically, environmentally and socially sustainable.

Bio Suisse: A Swiss national organization for organic-farming certification.

biodegradable: Anything that is capable of being decomposed by bacteria or other living organisms and thereby avoiding pollution.

biomimicry: The application of methods learned from the study of natural systems.

Blue Angel: A German national environmental labelling programme for the certification of products and services.

Bluesign: A Swiss organization for environmental standards in textile production.

burlap: see hessian.

carbon footprint: The amount of greenhouse gases emitted in a specific timeframe or in the production of a product.

carbon offsetting: Carbon offsetting allows you to compensate for your unavoidable emissions by helping to fund projects that deliver an equivalent carbon dioxide saving elsewhere, such as the planting of trees or investment in solar energy.

CERES: A US public code of environmental conduct aimed at integrating sustainability into capital markets for the health of the planet and its people.

certification: A system of standards for products, processes and trade, which is independently monitored.

chain stitch: The thread is looped around the needle to create a stitch with a chainlike appearance.

Clean Clothes Campaign: An alliance of organizations dedicated to improving working conditions in clothing manufacture.

Clean Production Action (CPA): An organization that designs and delivers strategic solutions for sustainable materials and environmentally preferable products.

clearcutting or clearfelling: Deforestation through logging.

Climate Project: Founded by Al Gore, this is a non-profit organization that educates the public and raises awareness about climate change.

compliance: A commitment to a self-determined code of conduct in business.

Control Union: A Dutch inspection and certification body, formerly known as SKAL, for agricultural and quality management systems.

Corporate Social Responsibility (CSR): A form of corporate self-regulation integrated into a business model.

CorpWatch: A non-profit investigative journal to expose corporate wrongdoing and to advocate multinational corporate accountability and transparency.

cotton wick: Loosely twisted cotton fibres that form a rope of various widths, traditionally used for gaslights and candlewicks, but also used in the garment industry for piping.

Cradle to Cradle Certification: A certification that measures achievement of eliminating waste in environmentally intelligent design.

Debio: A Norwegian organization that regulates the production and labelling of organic agricultural products.

downcycling: The process of recycling materials or products into new materials or products of lesser quality or reduced functionality.

drop needle rib: A knitted fabric that is produced by dropping a stitch in the knitting process to create a ribbed effect.

Earth Day Network: An educational website for the promotion of a healthy planet through education and activism.

Earth Pledge: A US voluntary partnership between businesses and governments to accelerate the adoption of sustainable practices.

Eco-Label: A European scheme designed to help consumers recognize environmentally friendly products and services of high quality.

ECOCERT: A French organic certification organization.

ecology: The study of the interactions between organisms and their physical environment.

ecosystem: A biological community of interdependent organisms that share a habitat.

environmental audit: An examination of a company's environmental impact.

Environmental Justice Foundation: An environmental charity to empower people who suffer from environmental abuses.

Ethical Fashion Forum: A not-for-profit network focusing on social and environmental sustainability in the fashion industry.

fair trade: A system whereby workers receive a fair and equitable living wage and benefits through employment.

Fairtrade Labelling Organizations International (FLO): An international non-profit association comprised of 24 organizations working to secure a better deal for producers.

felt: A non-woven fabric made from matting and pressing wool, generally through a process involving water, soap and hard work.

first hand: An industry term to describe the person who interprets a designer's sketch into the first sample.

Forest Stewardship Council (FSC): An international organization dedicated to responsible forestry management. It runs a global forest certification system.

FutureFashion: An initiative to help the fashion and home furnishing industries make the transition to sustainable materials.

Fuxicos: A type of patchwork made from circles of fabric gathered in the centre and patchworked together.

garment washing: A process of washing a whole garment to produce a washed effect in the final piece. It is usually creased and, dependent upon the fabric washed, can be moderately distressed.

Global Organic Textile Standard (GOTS): A standard that defines requirements to ensure the organic status of textiles, from growing and harvesting to manufacture and labelling.

Global Reporting Initiative (GRI): A network-based organization that has pioneered the development of the world's most widely used sustainability reporting framework.

global warming: The gradual increase in the overall temperature of the earth's atmosphere due to the greenhouse effect.

green: A common term referring to environmentally friendly processes.

greenhouse gases: Gases that absorb infrared radiation. They greatly affect the temperature of the earth and contribute to climate change and ozone destruction.

hand: An industry term that refers to the feel and drape of a fabric.

hessian: A rough woven fabric often used in sacks or for the back of carpets.

Human Rights Watch: An independent organization that defends and protects human rights.

ICE Compliance: A global independent auditing system for dye houses, printers, laundries and tanneries.

Ikat: A fabric woven from pre-dyed warp or weft threads, creating a pattern or design when woven.

Institute for Ethical and Environmental Certification (ICEA): An Italian organic certification body across multiple product sectors.

Institute for Marketecology (IMO): A European assurance and certification body for eco-friendly products and organic agriculture.

intaglio: A printmaking technique whereby a design is incised or engraved into a surface.

International Association of Natural Textile Industry (IVN): An international union of textile producers with strict ecological and social guidelines, working under the 'NatureTextil' label.

International Wool Textile Organization (IWTO): An international body representing the interests of the world's wool trade.

Isha Foundation: A volunteer-run non-profit organization dedicated to cultivating human potential.

Japanese Agricultural Standard (JAS): A regulating body for organic textile products.

Japanese Organic Cotton Association (JOCA): A non-profit organization for the certification, labelling and promotion of organic cotton products.

KRAV: A 28-member organic organization in Sweden and the Scandinavian countries that employs organic textile standards.

Labour Behind the Label: An organization that supports global garment workers' efforts to defend their rights.

Leadership in Energy and Environmental Design (LEED): A system that rates buildings on their environmental impact and effectiveness.

lifecycle: An industry term referring to the process of procurement, production and disposal of an item.

Lifestyles of Health and Sustainability (LOHAS): An index that rates goods and services in the areas of health, social justice, the environment and sustainable living.

Live Earth: A global movement using the power of entertainment to solve environmental issues.

Local Governments for Sustainability (ICLEI): An international association of governments working to advance sustainable development and climate protection.

lyocell: A cellulose (vegetable matter) fibre made from wood pulp, also known as Tencel, and noted for its durability, softness and eco-friendly manufacturing techniques.

MADE-BY: An independent label awarded for sustainable clothing production and aimed at expanding socially responsible production.

Made in Green: A symbol denoting overall quality for textile products, guaranteeing that they are free from substances harmful to health.

mono material: A material that is wholly comprised of a single material.

National Organic Program (NOP): A US accreditation body for the certification of organic agricultural products including textiles and clothing.

needle felt: A type of felting that integrates fleece into a woven textile base, through a jabbing motion using barbed needles.

No Sweat: An organization to fight sweatshop exploitation.

non-governmental organization (NGO): A non-profit group created to serve a social need and not representing or run by either a corporation or a government.

Nuno felting: A Japanese technique that melds fleece into a base fabric.

Oeko-Tex: A globally uniform testing and certification system for textiles.

OneCert: A European certifier of organic products and textiles.

Oregon Tilth: A non-profit research and educational organization for biological and socially equitable agriculture.

organic certification: A certification process for producers of organic food and other organic agricultural products. It is subject to strict legal guidelines and generally involves a set of production standards for growing, storage, processing, packaging and shipping.

Organic Exchange: A US charity committed to expanding organic agriculture, with a specific focus on increasing the production and use of organically grown fibres such as cotton.

organic farming: Farming without the use of chemical fertilizers, pesticides or other artificial chemicals.

peace silk: Silk fibre that is produced while allowing the silkworm to live out its full lifecycle. Also known as vegetarian silk.

People and Planet: A UK-based student-action organization campaigning to eradicate world poverty, defend human rights and protect the environment.

Pesticide Action Network (PAN): A non-profit organization working internationally to eliminate the dangers of toxic pesticides, our exposure to them and their presence in the environment.

photogram printing: An image is produced by placing an object on photosensitive paper and exposing it to light.

post-consumer waste: Products or materials that are discarded after use.

pre-consumer waste: Materials wasted through the production of a product, and discarded before it is ready for consumer use.

Programme for the Endorsement of Forest Certification (PEFC): An NGO that promotes sustainably managed forests through independent certification.

Recycling: The reuse of used materials for the same or another purpose, preventing waste and reducing consumption.

sasawashi: A fabric made from Japanese paper and kumazasa (a bamboo grass).

SeaCell®: A cellulose-based fibre made from seaweed.

selvedge: The self-finished edges of fabric that keep the fabric from fraying.

shantung: A woven fabric with uneven slubs in the weave, usually made from raw silk, but it can be simulated in other fibres.

shibori: A Japanese process of dyeing fabric with a pattern by gathering, folding or twisting to create little puckers in the fabric and a tie-dyed affect.

Sierra Club: An organization working to protect communities and the planet.

slub: A soft thick nub in yarn that is either an imperfection or purposely set for a desired effect.

Social Accountability International (SAI): An NGO whose mission is to advance the human rights of workers through a verification system.

Soil Association Certification: A UK organization that inspects and awards organic certification to farms and businesses that meet its organic standards.

stock-keeping unit (SKU): A unique identifier for each distinct product in a retail environment.

strike off: A test sample print, generally used for approval purposes only.

supply chain: The chain of people and companies that transforms raw materials into finished products.

sustainability: A system that is self-sustaining and does not pollute or need replenishment for its continued productivity, except by natural means.

sustainable development: Development that preserves the environment so as not to compromise the needs of current or future generations.

Swedish Society for Nature Conservation (SSNC): An environmental organization that spreads knowledge, maps environmental threats, creates solutions and runs an eco-labelling system for products.

tabi: An ankle-length, unisex, traditional Japanese sock that separates the big toe from the rest of the toes.

tanning: The process of taking a raw animal skin (which easily decomposes) and producing leather (which does not easily decompose), usually through the use of acidic chemical compounds such as lime, minerals and sodium sulphide.

Tearfund: A Christian relief and development agency.

Thanka, Thangka: A traditional Nepalese painted Buddhist banner hung in a monastery or family altar.

The GLOBE (Global Learning and Observations to Benefit the Environment) Program: Founded by Al Gore, GLOBE is a worldwide primary- and secondary-school–based science and education programme to investigate the environment and the earth.

The Textile Technology Institute (AITEX): A European non-profit organization and owner of the 'Made in Green' certification.

Trade Justice Movement: An umbrella group of organizations, unions, agencies and faith groups campaigning for trade justice, with the rules weighted to benefit poor people and the environment.

UN Global Compact: A United Nations initiative that seeks to promote responsible corporate citizenship in business.

United Nations Environment Programme (UNEP): A programme that provides leadership and encourages partnership in caring for the environment by inspiring and informing nations and peoples to improve their quality of life without compromising that of future generations.

upcycling: The process of converting or redesigning unwanted items or waste materials into something of equal or much better quality.

vegetable tanning: The process of taking a raw animal skin and producing leather in a traditional manner using vegetable agents instead of mineral or chemical ones.

walking: A felting term that refers to the laborious process of working the wool fibres with soap and water into a non-woven fabric.

War on Want: An agency that campaigns for human rights and against the root causes of global poverty, inequality and injustice.

whipstitch: A stitch that finishes edges or attaches two pieces of fabric.

World Fair Trade Organization (WFTO): A body that accredits organizations that demonstrate a 100% commitment to fair trade.

Worldwide Responsible Accredited Production (WRAP): An independent non-profit organization for the certification of humane and ethical manufacture throughout the world.

Zero Waste: A practice that encourages the reuse of all products to eliminate waste.

Resources

Books

Aburdene, Patricia, *Megatrends 2010: The Rise of Conscious Capitalism*, Hampton Roads Publishing Company, Charlottesville, VA, 2005.

Bierhals, Christine Anna, *Green Designed: Fashion*, AV Edition, Paris, 2008.

Black, Sandy, *Eco-Chic: The Fashion Paradox*, Black Dog Publishing, London, 2008.

Black, Sandy (ed), *Fashioning Fabrics: Contemporary Textiles in Fashion*, Black Dog Publishing, London, 2006.

Blanchard, Tamsin, *Green is the New Black: How to Change the World with Style*, Hodder & Stoughton, London, 2007.

Braungart, Michael and McDonough, William, *Cradle to Cradle: Remaking the Way We Make Things*, North Point Press, New York, 2002.

Brower, Cara and Mallory, Rachel, *Experimental EcoDesign*, RotoVision, Brighton, UK, 2005.

Fletcher, Kate, *Sustainable Fashion and Textiles: Design Journeys*, Earthscan, Sterling, UK, 2008.

Florida, Richard, *The Rise of the Creative Class*, Basic Books, New York, NY, 2002.

Fuad-Luke, Alastair, *The Eco-Design Handbook: A Complete Sourcebook for the Home and Office*, Thames & Hudson, London, 2002.

Hanaor, Ziggy (ed), introduction Lucy Siegle, *Recycle: The Essential Guide*, Black Dog Publishing, London, 2006.

Kaag, Ines and Heiss, Desiree (eds), *Bless. Celebrating 10 Years of Themelessness: No. 00–No. 29*, Sternberg Press, Berlin, 2006.

Klein, Naomi, *No Logo*, Picador, New York, NY, 2002.

Lee, Matilda, *Eco Chic: The Savy Shoppers Guide to Ethical Fashion*, Gaia Books, London, 2007.

Lynas, Mark, *Carbon Counter: Calculate Your Carbon Footprint*, Collins Gem, HarperCollins Publishers, London, 2007.

Minney, Safia, *By Hand: The Fair Trade Fashion Agenda*, People Tree Ltd, London, 2008.

Naik, Anita, *The Lazy Girl's Guide to Green Living*, Piatkus Books, London, 2007.

Poole, Buzz, (ed), *Green Design*, Mark Batty Publisher, New York, NY, 2006.

Quinn, Bradley, *Textile Designers at the Cutting Edge*, Laurence King Publishing, London, 2009.

Ray, Paul H. and Sherry Ruth Anderson, *The Cultural Creatives: How 50 Million People are Changing the World*, Harmony Books, New York, NY, 2001.

Rivoli, Pietra, *The Travels of a T-shirt in the Global Economy: An Economist Examines the Markets, Power and Politics of World Trade*, John Wiley & Sons, New Jersey, NJ, 2005.

Stop Climate Chaos Coalition, *I Count: Your Step-by-Step Guide to Climate Bliss. We Can Stop Climate Chaos*, Penguin Group, London, 2006.

Young European Fashion Designers, Daab gmbh, Cologne, Germany, 2008.

Films, documentaries and video clips

An Inconvenient Truth: A Global Warning, directed by Davis Guggenheim, Lawrence Bender Productions, 2006, www.climatecrisis.net

Fashion's Environmental Impact, by Howard Johnson, BBC news UK video, 21 February 2009, news.bbc.co.uk/2/hi/africa/7903079.stm

Fast Fashion from UK to Uganda, by Jack Garland, BBC news UK article and video, 20 February 2009, news.bbc.co.uk/2/hi/uk_news/7899227.stm?lss

The Age of Stupid, directed and written by Franny Armstrong, Spanner Films, 2009, www.ageofstupid.net

The Corporation, directed by Mark Achbar and Jennifer Abbott, written by Joel Bakan, Big Picture Media Corporation, 2003, www.thecorporation.com

Trouble the Water, directed by Carl Deal and Tia Lessin, Elsewhere Films, 2008, www.troublethewaterfilm.com

Websites

Adore Vintage: A website selling vintage fashions, www.adorevintage.com

A Lot of Organics: A UK organic search engine for a broad range of ecological and ethical products, www.alotoforganics.co.uk

Branch: A website selling ecological interior products, www.branchhome.com

Coco's Shoppe: A website selling ecological fashions and products, cocosshoppe.com/store

Couture Lab: A website selling luxury fashion and accessories, www.couturelab.com

Curbly: A community website and blog featuring a range of artists working in various mediums, including some sustainable design, www.curbly.com

Dandelion Vintage: An online vintage reseller, www.dandelionvintage.com

Envi be Green: A website selling eco-fashion labels, www.shopenvi.com

Etsy: A website selling handmade or vintage products for all occasions, www.etsy.com/index.php

FiftyRx3: An ethical website and blog, fiftyrx3.blogspot.com

Freecycle: A website through which local people give or receive items for free to keep things out of landfill, www.freecycle.org

Global Cool: A magazine-style site with fun ideas on how to reduce the emission of greenhouse gases, www.globalcool.org

Green with Glamour: A style website and blog selling eco-friendly design, www.greenwithglamour.com

Grist: An online environmental commentary and advice service, www.grist.org

Inhabitat: A website and blog tracking sustainable innovations in technology, practices and materials, www.inhabitat.com

Living Green: A website selling ecological interior and exterior products for the home, www1.livingreen.com

Not Just a Label: A website for new designers with a sustainable rating, www.notjustalabel.com

Original Women: A website and store based around ethical accessories and products, shop.original-women.com

People Tree: A website selling ecological fashions and accessories, peopletree.co.uk

Reusable Bags: An online information site about recyclable bags, www.reusablebags.com

Style Will Save Us: A digital magazine for a green lifestyle, www.stylewillsaveus.com

Sublime: A sustainable lifestyle magazine, sublimemagazine.com

Swap-a-Rama Razzmatazz: A website that organizes clothes-swapping parties, www.swap-a-rama.co.uk

The Green Guide for Everyday Living: National Geographic's guide to sustainable living, www.thegreenguide.com

The New Consumer: A UK webzine on ethical lifestyles, www.newconsumer.com

Treehugger: A webzine promoting mainstream sustainability, www.treehugger.com

What's Mine is Yours: A website for swapping, selling or buying clothes and furniture, www.whatsmineisyours.com

Index

Picture credits

The publisher and author would like to thank the following companies and individuals for permission to reproduce images in this book. In all cases, every effort has been made to credit the copyright holders, but should there be any omissions or errors the publisher would be pleased to insert the appropriate acknowledgement in any subsequent edition of this book. L=left, R=right, T=top, B=bottom, C=centre:

p2: courtesy of FIN
p7: courtesy of Geoffrey B. Small; TR, C: photo by Pierre Gayte Paris
p8L: Elena García – Hannah Radley-Bennett 2008, www.hannahradleybennett.com, model Erica Rodriguez, www.ericarodriguez.com; TR: courtesy of FIN; C: ModaFusion – photo by Ricardo Fasanello
p10L: Elena García – Nick Fallon, www.nickfallon.net; TR: Camilla Norrback – photo by Ann-Katrin Blomquist; C: Royah Atelier – photo by Marco Valerio Esposito
p13: Shoto Banerji – photo by Sion Parkinson
pp14–17: Alabama Chanin – photos by Robert Rausch 2008, www.gasdesigncenter.com
pp18–21: Amana – photos by Amarpaul Kalirai
pp22–23: El Naturalista; p22: photo by Vincente Paredes; p23: photos by Anna Marti
pp24–25: Elena García – Hannah Radley-Bennett, www.hannahradleybennett.com
pp26–29: courtesy of Leila Hafzi; pp26R–29: photos by Emile Ashley, Ashley Studio
pp30–31: Les Fées de Bengale – photos by Julien Caidos, model Juliette Doll
pp32–33: ModaFusion; p32: courtesy of Nadine Gonzalez; p33: photos by Ricardo Fasanello
pp34–35: Mona Mohanna – Lidia Bagnara Fotografa, lidiabagnara@interfee.it, courtesy of Mona Mohanna, monamohanna@yahoo.it
pp36–39: Noir; p36: photo Ole Lund; p37: photos by Marc Hom; p38: photo by Sacha Maric: p39T: photo by Marc Hom; B: photo by Ole Lund
pp40–41: Royah – photos by Marco Valerio Esposito
pp42–45: courtesy of sense-organics; pp43–45: photos by Phillip Jeker, DAA Photos and Nico Beckmann, models Lars Weber, Katja Matthes, Larissa Rausch, Phillip Wiedemann, Sarah Maria Besgen & Rote Rosen
pp46–47: Shoto Banerji; p46: photos by Preeti Bedi; p47T: photo by Sion Parkinson; p47B: courtesy of Shoto Banerji
pp48–51: Taller Flora – photos by Mark Powell, courtesy of Carla Fernandez
pp53–56: Van Markoviec; p53: photo by Magda Lipiejko, model Ewelina, ML Studio; pp54–55: photo by Magda Lipiejko, model Sylwia, ML Studio
p56: Camilla Norrback – photo by Ann-Katrin Blomquist
pp58–61: Alexandra Faro – photos by Guy Stephens
pp62–65: Camilla Norrback – photos by Ann-Katrin Blomquist
pp66–69: Céline Faizant – photos by Matthieu Granier
pp70–73: courtesy of Christine Birkle
pp74–75: Ciel – photos by Ben Gold, ben@bengold.co.uk

pp76–77: Emily Katz; p76: photos by Holly Stalder; p77: photos by Joshua Jay Elliott
pp78–79: Enamore – photos by Thomas Martin, hair and make-up Maddie Austin
pp80–81: courtesy of FIN
pp82–83: Françoise Hoffmann – photos by Anna Sole
pp84–87: Linda Loudermilk – photos by David Casteel
pp88–92: Magdalena Schaffrin; p89: photos by Mischa Heintze, make-up Ines Schult;
pp90–91: photos by Marcus Lapp
pp92–93: Royal Blush – photos by Nicolas Henri, www.nicolashenri.ch, make-up and hair by Nadia Smug, styling by Jana Keller, model Fotogen
pp94–95: Samant Chauhan – photos by Ragubeer Singh
pp96–97: U Roads – art direction by Gaetano Curci, styling by Bruno Bordese. Trading – The DC Company
pp98–101: Yoj – photos by Aldo Castoldi
p102: Demano – photo by Juan Antonio Monsalve
pp104–105: Angela Johnson – photos by David H. Smith, models Marissa Rham, Frances Moeller, Dominique Garino Mackler & Jillian Rham, hair and make-up by Cherelynn Baker, styling by Veronica Sahwany and Shannon Campbell
pp106–107: Costumisée par Liza; T: photo by Sacha Goldberger; B: photo by Neo Tony Lee
pp108–109: Demano – photos by Juan Antonio Monsalve
pp110–111: E2 – courtesy of Couturelab Limited
pp112–113: Frau Wagner – photos by Anja Bleyl, graphics by Frau Wagner Grafics
pp114–117: From Somewhere – photos by Geoffrey Grunfeld
pp118–121: Geoffrey B. Small; p118: photos by Pierre Gayte Paris; pp119–121: photos by Guido Barbagelata – courtesy of Geoffrey B. Small
pp122–123: courtesy of Josh Jakus
pp124–125: Preloved; p124: photo by Lise Varrette; pp125–127: photos by Jordan Eady, www.jordaneady.com
pp128–129: Rebound Designs – photos by Pete Duvall, Anything Photographic
pp130–131: Riedizioni – photos by Piero Gemelli
pp132–133: Stephan Hann – photos by Itai Margula
pp134–134: Suitcase – photos by Robert Berry
pp136–139: TRAIDremade; p136T: photo by Mike Blackett; p136B, p137T: photos by Alessandra Rigillo; p137B, pp138–139: photos by Mike Blackett
p140: courtesy of Rebecca Earley – photo by Oliver Reed
pp142–145: aforest-design; p143, 144T, p145: photos by Rui Vasco, Arquivo Moda Lisboa; p144B: courtesy of aforest-design
pp146–149: Andrea Zittel, courtesy of Andrea Rosen Gallery, New York
pp150–151: Bless – courtesy of Bless
pp152–153: Collection of Hope – photo Amin Akhtar
pp154–157: Holly McQuillan; pp154–155: photos by Thomas McQuillan
pp158–161: Mark Liu; p158: photo by Ela

Hawes, styling Katie Burnett, model Lin Levala, Premier modeling agency; p159: photo by Patrick Camara Ropeta, model Eleanor Griffiths; p160R, p161: photos by Patrick Camara Ropeta, model Eleanor Griffiths; p160L: courtesy of Mark Liu
pp162–163: Nau; p162T: photo by Swanson Studio; p162B, p163T, B: Daniel Sharp Photography 2008; C: photo by by Ben Moon
pp164–167: Rebecca Earley & Kate Goldsworthy – courtesy of B. Earley; p165: photo by Oliver Reed; p166: photo by Tom Gidley; p167: courtesy of Kate Goldsworthy
pp168–169: Redesign the World – courtesy of Cornelia Bamert
p170: Phillipe Starck – courtesy of Starck Network
pp172–173: Agatha Ruiz de la Prada – courtesy of yoox.com
pp174–175: courtesy of Barneys New York
pp176–179: H&M Designers Against AIDS; pp176–178: photos by Daniel Jackson; p179: Anouck Lepere, photo by Marc Lagrange; www.designersagainstaids.com
pp180–183: Katherine Hamnett; p180: photo by Alex Sturrock, model Rhys Thomas; p181: photo by Alex Sturrock, models Jen Dawson & Kofi; pp182–183: photos by Alex Sturrock, model Rebecca Pearson
pp184–187: Miguel Adrover – courtesy of Hessnatur
pp188–189: Phillipe Starck – courtesy of Starck Network
pp190–191: Salvatore Ferragamo – courtesy of Salvatore Ferragamo Italia SpA
pp192–195: Vivienne Westwood – photos by Christopher Moore, Catwalking
pp196–199: Yeohlee Teng – photos by Dan Lecca
pp200–201: Yves Saint Laurent – courtesy of Barneys New York

Contacts

Author's acknowledgements

Thank you to all the designers featured in this my first book, who allowed me access to their studios, press galleries and took the time to answer my oft times pedestrian questions, as well as patiently accept my disorganization, ongoing persistence and sometime annoyance. Nau were gracious enough to receive me at their head office in Portland, Oregon, for almost an entire day, putting their work on hold to play host to what was then a Masters student writing her graduate thesis. Luisa Cevese of Riedizioni kindly received me at her studio in Milan, as did Edson Raupe in London. Gabi of Royah Designs, of whom I became an instant friend and admirer after she played host to me at the first Ethical Show in Milan. Geoffrey B. Small shared an incredible amount of information with me, while granting a rare insight into his work and ethics; both an honor and a pleasure. His work is inspiring and his commitment to sustainability awesome, I can only hope not to embarrass him, and to some degree fulfill the trust he has shown in me, with my short coverage of his work that doesn't begin to do him justice.

Two organizations stand out above others due to their willingness to share information with me and promote friends, colleagues and competitors; Silvia Massimino of Ethical Press and Magdalena Schaffrin and Jana Keller of GREENshowroom, all of whom shared their contacts with me simply in an effort to promote green design, introducing me to countless designers.

The sense of collaboration in this area of design is heart warming and in no small way renews my faith in the fashion industry. I am proud to play whatever small part I can in the promotion of eco design.

Thank you to my friends, who supported and encouraged me, and sent me snippets of information. Thank you especially to Renee, Joshua and David, always David. Finally thank you to my editor, Zoe Antoniou and to Helen Rochester, the commissioning Editor at Laurence King, as well as Catherine Hooper, copy editor – without all of whose generosity of spirit and unending patience and faith, this book would never have reached completion. Thank you.